REMEMBERING TRADITIONAL HANZI

Remembering Simplified Hanzi: How Not to Forget the Meaning and Writing of Chinese Characters, Book 1. Honolulu: University of Hawai'i Press, 2009

Remembering Simplified Hanzi: How Not to Forget the Meaning and Writing of Chinese Characters, Book 2. Honolulu: University of Hawai'i Press, 2012

Remembering Traditional Hanzi: How Not to Forget the Meaning and Writing of Chinese Characters, Book 1. Honolulu: University of Hawai'i Press, 2009

Remembering Traditional Hanzi

How Not to Forget the Meaning and Writing of Chinese Characters

Book 2

James W. Heisig

Timothy W. Richardson

University of Hawai'i Press
HONOLULU

17 16 15 14 13 12   6 5 4 3 2 1

Library of Congress Cataloging-in-Publication Data

Heisig, James W., 1944- Remembering traditional Hanzi : book 2 : how not to forget the
meaning and writing of Chinese characters / James W. Heisig, Timothy W. Richardson.
    p. cm. Includes indexes. ISBN 978-0-8248-3324-4 (pbk. : alk. paper)
    1. Chinese Characters. 2. Chinese language--Study and teaching. I. Richardson,
    Timothy W. II. Title. III. Title: How not to forget the meaning and writing of
    Chinese characters.
PL1171.H45 2008 495.1'07—dc22   2008033030

Remembering Traditional Hanzi: Book 2
ISBN 978-0-8248-3656-6

The typesetting for this book was done at the Nanzan Institute for Religion and Culture.

University of Hawai'i Press books are printed on acid-free paper and meet the guidelines
for permanence and durability of the Council on Library Resources.

CONTENTS

INTRODUCTION

THIS IS THE second of two volumes designed to help students with the meaning and writing of the 3,000 most frequently used traditional Chinese characters. A parallel set of volumes has been prepared for simplified characters. Although there is considerable overlap in the selection and arrangement of the characters, as well as in the mnemonic devices employed, you are advised to stick with one set of books or the other. As we explained in the Introduction to Book 1, combining your learning of traditional and simplified characters is likely to slow down progress and create confusion. That Introduction also provides further details about the approach followed in these books and the rationale behind it.

HOW TO USE THIS BOOK

From the start, our working assumption was that Book 1 and Book 2 would be studied *sequentially*. Each book would introduce half of the most important 3,000 characters in the Chinese language. The idea was that since the 1,000 most frequently used characters were to be introduced in Book 1, learners would complete that volume before passing on to the second. Many, if not most, students will find this preferable.

However, as we weighed the options for organizing the remaining 1,500 characters for Book 2, we realized that others may prefer the more exacting, but also more rationally satisfying, approach of studying the two volumes *simultaneously*. We have adjusted the Introduction to Book 1 to clarify the reasons why this is so, but a word of explanation is in order here.

As each new primitive was presented in Book 1, most of the characters (among the 1,500 selected for the first volume) that could be learned at that point were introduced. The lessons of Book 2 have been designed as extensions of that principle. Thus, nearly all of the 1,500 characters of Book 2 are placed in the lessons in which they *would have appeared* if we had combined everything into a single volume. This means that students who wish to do so can treat the corresponding lessons of Books 1 and 2 as single units.

Having said this, we hasten to add a note of caution: Book 1 was designed to progress from complete stories to short plots to the simple listing of a character's primitive elements. In this way, the student gradually gains independence

1

from the imagination of the authors and develops a knack for creating stories based on personal memories and learning preferences. Book 2 disregards this progression. Even in the early pages, one will find mere plots and listings of elements where the lessons of Book 1 would have given more information. Occasionally we supply a fuller story to clarify the connotation of a key word or to help with a particularly challenging character—or sometimes simply because we cannot resist the temptation. But these are the exception.

Accordingly, if you wish to study the books simultaneously, you may want to get several lessons into Book 1 before you crack Book 2, and then return to those lessons to pick up the new characters.

COMPOUNDS, POSTSCRIPTS, INDEXES

The 55 lessons of this book are followed by a short special section with "compounds" or characters that are best learned in pairs. A final section contains two "postscripts" that we strongly urge you not to skip over.

The Indexes of Book 2 differ slightly from those of Book 1. Index 1 gives a hand-drawn character and its pronunciation for each frame in Book 2. The other four Indexes are comprehensive. That is, they cover the relevant information from both volumes. This will make it easier for you to navigate all 3,000 characters without the need to consult the Indexes from Book 1.

It bears repeating that the pronunciations given in the Indexes are given as an aid should you need to consult a dictionary. Nothing further is said about them in these volumes, and no examples of their use are provided. As we recommended in the Introduction to Book 1, it is best to study the writing and meaning of the characters separately from their pronunciation.

ON CHARACTERS AND THEIR KEY WORDS

Finding unique English key words for 3,000 different Chinese characters was challenging in the extreme. Often there is more than one ordinary character in Chinese corresponding to a single word in English. At times this left us no choice but to stretch the limits of standard English ever so slightly, employing common phrases or even neologisms in order to avoid the duplication of key words. In any case, if you follow the guidance given along the way about preserving a distinct connotation for each key word and heeding its part of speech, these hurdles will be easy to hop over.

Although we do not draw attention to the fact in each case, a relatively small number of the characters presented in the lessons are "bound forms." That is, much like the "compounds" that are given their own section, these characters are always used in combination with others. The Chinese equivalents of "trumpet," "glaze," and "universe," for example, are usually considered to be two-character compounds. Nevertheless, our policy has been to assign each individual character its own key word on the assumption that when the time comes for students to learn compounds, they will find it a straightforward task. Take "trumpet," for instance: the character with that key word (FRAME 1501) is often paired in a compound with that for "flared horn" (2584) to designate what English simply calls a "trumpet."

Remember, too, that while some key words carry clear and discrete connotations, others can only approximate the range of meanings and nuances covered by a character. A broader awareness of what individual characters convey can only be acquired by encountering them in context over time.

A final note of caution: We urge you to avoid dismissing certain characters as not being very useful simply because their key words are not ones you run into very often. "Lambsquarters" and "water caltrops" are not part of everyday English vocabulary, and never appear in personal or family names. Things are different in the world of the characters. It is safe to assume that if a character appears in these books, you will need it to gain proficiency in Chinese.

ACKNOWLEDGMENTS

The authors would like to reiterate their thanks to Robert Roche for his insight, encouragement, and generous assistance over the long years this project has been in the works. The staff and fellows of the Nanzan Institute for Religion and Culture in Nagoya, Japan, made our task a lot easier and provided just the right atmosphere for collaboration. Thanks, too, to Brigham Young University–Hawaii for its support of the project. Tsu-Pin Huang, Yifen Beus, and Pao-Ho Wan assisted us with their expertise on numerous occasions. Pat Crosby, Keith Leber, and Nadine Little of University of Hawai'i Press deserve mention for patiently seeing this book through its editing and production. A special word of appreciation is due Helen Richardson and the Richardson children. Without their willingness to make do without a husband and father for weeks at a time, concentrated periods of work in Japan over the past several years would not have been possible.

Finally, we wish to acknowledge the many readers who have sent us their comments, reactions, and suggestions since the appearance of Book 1. Their feedback has not only made for important improvements; it has confirmed our confidence that we are on the right track.

James W. Heisig
Timothy W. Richardson
15 July 2011

Lessons

Lesson 1

As explained in the Introduction, the lessons of Book 2 are organized according to the characters and primitives introduced in their corresponding lesson in Book 1. With that, we start Book 2 off with a blast:

1501   trumpet [N.]

叭 Since the character *eight* depicts an open expanse that begins in the heavens and covers the earth, it is just right for the character that shows the Angel Gabriel pressing his *mouth* against the **trumpet** to announce the end of time—or in this case, the end of Lesson 1. [5]

丶   口   口   叨   叭

LESSON 2

THERE IS only one new character we can make with the elements from Lesson 2 of Book 1.

1502	mutter

咕   Since we already used the image of an *ancient* tombstone in Lesson 2 of Book 1 and we have the *mouth* on the left, we need only think of someone trying to **mutter** something to us. Perhaps it's someone that would like to be let out. [8]

口   咕

Lesson 3

1503 **we (inclusive)**

咱

Mouth . . . nostrils. Chinese is one of those languages (Indonesian is another) that have two different ways of expressing "**we**," one including the person or persons spoken to, the other excluding them. We will meet the latter in FRAME 2032. [9]

口　咱

1504 **string together**

串

This character looks like a doodle of a shish kebab. Can you see the skewer used to **string together** those tasty little tidbits for grilling over the fire? Identifying a character by it shape rather than by its primitive elements is something we have shied away from, but we think you will agree this one merits treating as an exception. [7]

口　吕　串

1505 **overspread** (v.)

罩

Just as awnings, clouds, and bedspreads cover things, the *net* in this character is used to **overspread** an *eminent* person, probably the only way to capture his attention. [13]

罒　罩

LESSON 4

1506   hubbub

囂

So what is all the **hubbub** about? Look for yourself: four *mouths gathered around a table and* munching away noisily on—a *head!* (In FRAME 230 it is a chihuahua.) [21]

吅   貥   囂

LESSON 5

YOU WILL notice that in most cases only the primitive elements are given below, without any detailed story or story plot. Book 1 progresses from full stories to simple plots to component elements. The idea is to gradually turn more and more of the creative work over to the learner. If you feel you are not quite ready to venture off on your own at this point but still want to study the two books together, you might hold off on the lessons of Book 2 until later, when you are more comfortable with inventing your own images and stories.

1507 顛	*True . . . head.* [19]	真 顛	invert
1508 叨	*Mouth . . . dagger.* [5]	口 叨	talkative
1509 刮	*Tongue . . . saber.* [8]	舌 刮	scrape (v.)
1510 盯	*Eyeballs . . . nail.* [7]	目 盯	stare at
1511 呵	*Mouth . . . can.* [8]	口 呵	rebuke (v.)

LESSON 6

1512 姦	Three *women.* [9] 女　姦　姦	adultery
1513 嬰	Two *oysters . . . woman.* [17] 貝　賏　嬰	baby
1514 姑	*Woman . . . ancient.* [8] 女　姑	father's sister
1515 姆	*Woman . . . mother.* [8] 女　姆	nanny
1516 兢	*Overcome . . . overcome.* [14] 克　兢	cautious

LESSON 7

1517	big
碩	To remember this character, you need only think of those **big** *stone heads* found in Mesoamerica or on Easter Island. [14]
	石　碩

1518	lay brick
砌	*Stone . . . cut.* [9]
	石　砌

1519	whistle [N.]
哨	*Mouth . . . candle.* [10]
	口　哨

1520	sway [V.]
晃	*Sun . . . ray.* [10]
	日　晃

LESSON 8

1521	moor ^(v.)

1521   moor [v.]

泊   *Water . . . dove.* [8]

氵　泊

1522   get rid of

汰   What you **get rid of** in this character is a house plant that has been *overly watered.* [7]

氵　汰

1523   soak

沾   *Water . . . tell fortunes.* When you hear this key word, think of how a thundershower **soaks** you to the skin, not of something left to **soak** overnight in a marinade. [8]

氵　沾

1524   insignificant

渺   This key word connotes small or trifling. Its elements: *water . . . eyeball . . . few.* [12]

氵　汨　渺

1525   gland

腺   *Flesh . . . spring.* [13]

月　腺

1526   level (ADJ.)

坦   The key word can refer both to **level** land and to those calm and
     composed people who always seem to keep themselves on an
     even keel. The elements: *soil . . . daybreak.* [8]

                            土   坦

1527   newborn (N.)

娃   *Woman . . . bricks.* This rather peculiar combination of ele-
     ments gives us the character for **newborns** of all kinds, human
     and animal. [9]

                            女   娃

1528   bank (N.)

涯   The **bank** shown here is a *cliff* of *bricks* meant to hold back the
     water. [11]

                       氵   沪   涯

1529   inch

吋   The addition of a *mouth* to a *Chinese inch* gives us a Western
     inch. [6]

                            口   吋

1530   elbow (N.)

肘   *Flesh . . . glued to.* [7]

                            月   肘

1531   scorch

灼   *Fire . . . ladle.* [7]

                            火   灼

1532		stir-fry [v.]
炒	Fire . . . few. [8]	
	火 炒	

1533		sprinkle
澆	Water . . . Pigpen. [15]	
	氵 澆	

LESSON 9

1534	mile
哩	*Mouth . . . computer.* [10]
	口　哩

1535	carp [N.]
鯉	*Fish . . . computer.* [18]
	魚　鯉

1536	Hey!
嘿	*Mouth . . . black.* [15]
	口　嘿

1537	cinnabar red
丹	*Hood . . . a drop . . . one.* This character, commonly used for the color red, is also an essential ingredient in Chinese alchemy. Note that the first stroke of *hood* curves slightly outward. [4]
	丿　刀　月　丹

1538	boisterous
喧	*Mouth . . . proclaim.* [12]
	口　喧

1539	visitor
賓	Dangling from the *ceiling* of your *house* are a *few shells*, the start of a hanging mobile on which you plan to hang trinkets you gather (surreptitiously or otherwise) from each **visitor** who comes. Nice conversation piece.

In FRAME 104 we warned that the final stroke of *few* might be eliminated when the primitive is cramped for space, as it is here. [14]

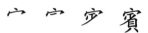

1540   water's edge

濱   *Water . . . visitor.* [17]

1541   widowed

寡   *House . . . head . . . dagger.* Here we have another instance of a very odd exception. Notice how the final stroke of the *head* is lengthened, giving the final two strokes a chance to stretch out and make room for the *dagger* that fits in beneath. But the real question is: Does the *dagger* in fact belong to the woman who was left **widowed** when her husband mysteriously lost his *head* in their *house*? [14]

广　宕　寡

Lesson 10

1542 棚	**shed** (N.)
	Tree . . . companion. [12]
	朩　棚

1543 柏	**cypress**
	Tree . . . dove. [9]
	朩　柏

1544 槙	**thick stick**
	Tree . . . tribute. Don't think of shillelagh or truncheon here, but of a **thick stick** used for less violent purposes. [14]
	朩　槙

1545 朵	**flouds**
	Since English does not have a "measure word" or "classifier" for flowers and clouds to go with this character, we shall just have to invent one: **flouds**. Its primitives are: wind . . . tree. [6]
	几　朵

1546 杜	**prevent**
	Tree . . . soil. [7]
	朩　杜

1547   cassia-bark tree

桂

The bark of the **cassia-bark tree**, akin to that of the cinnamon tree, is used as a spice. Its elements: *tree . . . bricks.* [10]

木 桂

1548   chair

椅

Tree . . . strange. [12]

木 椅

1549   hero

杰

Tree . . . cooking fire. [8]

木 杰

1550   cherry

櫻

The *baby* on this particular *tree* is a ripe, red **cherry** just waiting to be picked. [21]

木 櫻

1551   treetops

梢

Tree . . . candle. [11]

木 梢

1552   paulownia

桐

Since you probably don't know what a **paulownia** *tree* is, we shall let the key word suggest the phrase "the Little Brothers of St. **Paulownia.**" It is a short step to associate the *tree* with the *monks* to its right. (For the curious, the name of this oriental *tree* really comes from a Russian princess, Anna Pavlovna.) [10]

木 桐

1553 宋	Song
	This character refers to the **Song** Dynasty (960–1279). Its elements: *house . . . tree.* [7]

宀 宋

1554 淋	drench
	Water . . . woods. [11]

氵 淋

1555 焚	burn (v.)
	Woods . . . fire. [12]

林 焚

1556 昧	obscure (ADJ./V.)
	Sun . . . not yet. [9]

日 昧

1557 朱	vermilion
	That red-orange color we call vermilion is found in nature during the fall when the leaves lose their sugar and begin to change color. This character depicts the very last leaf on a tree in the fall (the *drop* hung on the first stroke), the leaf that has *not yet* fallen as it one day must. Look at its color—**vermilion**. (Well, not really. The truth is, **vermilion** is made from a mercuric sulfide, but we're sure you will agree that autumn leaves are a lot easier to work with.) [6]

丿 朱

1558 株	tree trunk
	Tree . . . vermilion. [10]

木　株

1559　　　　　　　　　　　　　　　　　　　　　　roof beam

樑　*Tree . . . water . . . blade . . . a drop . . . tree.* [15]

木　杚　柳　柳　柳　樑

1560　　　　　　　　　　　　　　　　　　　　　　saucer

碟　*Stone . . . family tree. If it is any help, this character is also used in the term for flying* **saucers**. [14]

石　碟

1561　　　　　　　　　　　　　　　　　　　　　　bud [v.]

萌　*Flowers . . . bright.* [12]

艹　萌

1562　　　　　　　　　　　　　　　　　　　　　　exacting

苛　*Flowers . . . can.* [9]

艹　苛

1563　　　　　　　　　　　　　　　　　　　　　　membrane

膜　*Flesh . . . graveyard.* [15]

月　膜

1564　　　　　　　　　　　　　　　　　　　　　　solitary

寞　*House . . . graveyard/nobody. We have included the key-word meaning of the second primitive as an alternative you might find useful. Remember, this is always a possibility.* [14]

宀　寞

1565   sunset

暮   *Graveyard . . . sun.* [15]

       艹   苜   莫   暮

LESSON 11

IF YOU ARE going through these Lessons in tandem with Book 1, you will probably have noticed that the new characters presented here are arranged in the same order they would have had in Book 1, namely, the order in which the primitive elements, or characters serving as primitive elements, have been introduced.

1566 燃	*Fire . . . sort of thing.* [16]	ignite

火　燃

1567 咒	*Chatterbox . . . wind.* [8]	curse [v.]

吅　咒

1568 獸	*Chatterbox . . . brains . . . floor . . . mouth . . . chihuahua.* [19]	beast

吅　畄　嘼　嘼　獸

1569 狸	*Pack of wild dogs . . . computer.* [10]	raccoon dog

犭　狸

1570 嗅	*Mouth . . . stinking.* [13]	sniff [v.]

口　嗅

1571

牡

dude

We already met a character to which we assigned the key word *male* (FRAME 691), but there are certain animals that use a different character for gender identification of the masculine variety. Animals like the **dude** deer (also known as the stag), the **dude** horse (alias, the stallion) and the **dude** cow (a.k.a, the bull) use it. It is composed of the primitive elements *cow* and *soil*. [7]

牛　牡

1572

牢

jail

House . . . cow. [7]

宀　牢

1573

贊

succor (v.)

An Oxford don is drowning in the local swimming pool and calls out "**Succor! Succor!**" After consulting their dictionaries, the lifeguards proceed to save the poor chap. Now instead of the typical lifesaver you find at poolside, they grab a giant *oyster* they have trained to swim out, grab hold of drowning swimmers, and drag them back to safety. When you launch it into the deep, you throw it like a discus and shout, *"Before! Before!"* to warn people to get out of the way, obviously a courtesy inherited from the golf course. [19]

先　兟　贊

❖ When used as a primitive element, this character will mean a *lifesaver*, in line with the explanation above.

1574	abode
舍	*Meeting . . . ancient.* [8]

へ 舍

1575	wha?
啥	This character is a colloquial abbreviation, often used in Internet communications, for the ordinary compound meaning "What?" Its elements: *mouth . . . abode.* [11]

口 啥

1576	in agreement
洽	*Water . . . fit.* [9]

氵 洽

1577	thriving
旺	When a *king* is **thriving**, the *sun* should be shining on his kingdom, but more often than not, it is just shining on HIM. As legends around the world remind us, what invariably happens to *kings* **thriving** at the expense of others is that they get consumed by their own selfishness—or, in the case of this character, *sun*-burned to a crisp until they decide that their subjects should be **thriving**, too. [8]

日 旺

1578	green jade
碧	*Jewel . . . dove . . . stone.* [14]

王　珀　碧

1579	tearful

汪　　*Water . . . jewels.* [7]

氵　汪

1580	crooked

枉　　*Tree . . . king.* This character usually applies to someone who bends the rules or perverts the law. [8]

木　枉

1581	pearl

珠　　*Jewel . . . vermilion.* [10]

王　珠

1582	shocking

噩　　*King . . . . four mouths.* [16]

一　丁　吋　吘　平　罪　䍂　噩

1583	crocodile

鱷　　*Fish . . . shocking.* If you are more familiar with *alligators* than **crocodiles**, feel free to adjust the key word accordingly. [27]

魚　鱷

1584	fight [v.]

鬥　　This character shows two old geezers having at it, each of them wielding a *walking stick* with a spiked *ball* on the end. They have been driven to **fight** for the title of king of the hill at the local retirement center. [10]

丨 𦥯 𦥯 鬥

1585

栓   plug (N.)

Tree . . . whole. [10]

木 栓

1586

柱   pillar

Tree . . . candlestick. [9]

木 柱

1587

鉤   hook (N./V.)

Metal . . . sentence. Be sure not to confuse this key word with the primitive element of the same meaning. [13]

金 鉤

1588

鈔   paper money

Metal . . . few. [12]

金 鈔

1589

銷   put up for sale

Gold . . . candle. [15]

金 銷

1590

鎖   lock (N./V.)

Metal . . . small . . . shell. [18]

金 𨦇 鎖

1591

鑽   drill (N./V.)

This key word for this character refers to the machine **drill** and has nothing to do with mental or physical exercises. Its elements: *metal . . . lifesaver.* [27]

金   鑽

LESSON 13

1592   **compel**

迫

To **compel** people to go somewhere they really don't want to go, the unscrupulous don't think twice about *white*washing the *road* to make it more appealing. [8]

白 迫

1593   **press** (v.)

逼

Wealth . . . road. The key word is used to describe the action of hounding someone or forcing them to do something. [12]

畐 逼

1594   **escape** (v.)

逃

There is no way to **escape** from this *portent*, which is seated smack in the middle of the *road* you are using to run away. [9]

兆 逃

1595   **flaunt**

逞

Submit . . . road. [10]

呈 逞

1596   **rumble** (N./V.)

轟

Three cars. [21]

車 軍 轟

1597   **rails**

軌

Car . . . baseball team. The kind of **rails** this character refers to are those used for train tracks, not for banisters. [9]

車 軌

1598   **flatten**

軋

Car . . . fishhook. [8]

車 軋

1599   **spokes**

輻

Car . . . wealth. [16]

車 輻

1600   **sauté** (v.)

煎

In front . . . cooking fire. [13]

前 煎

1601   **figure of speech**

喻

Analogies, similes, metaphors, and other **figures of speech** often serve a biting wit, depicted colorfully here as a *slaughterhouse mouth*. Nice **figure of speech**, eh? [12]

口 喻

1602   **elm**

榆

Tree . . . slaughterhouse. [13]

木 榆

1603

略

abbreviation

Each field has its own **abbreviations** (chemistry, philosophy, sports, etc.). Needless to say, the "stronger" primitive—that is to say, the simpler and more often used one—takes the dominant position on the left, even though the story would read them off the other way around. [11]

田

Lesson 14

As we do frequently in Book 1, from this point on we will occasionally assign new primitive meanings to characters you have already learned with a different key-word meaning. In many cases, some of the characters in which this new meaning is used will not appear until a later lesson. Each new primitive meaning will get its own frame, marked with the usual symbol (❖). The number in curly brackets refers to the frame number of the original character. We will introduce one such example in this lesson.

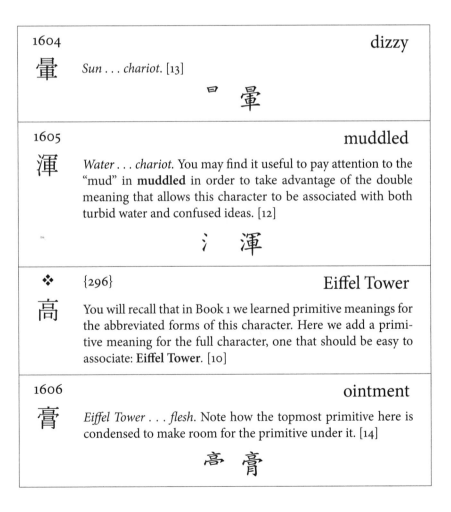

1604		dizzy
暈	*Sun . . . chariot.* [13]	
	曰　暈	

1605		muddled
渾	*Water . . . chariot.* You may find it useful to pay attention to the "mud" in **muddled** in order to take advantage of the double meaning that allows this character to be associated with both turbid water and confused ideas. [12]	
	氵　渾	

❖	{296}	Eiffel Tower
高	You will recall that in Book 1 we learned primitive meanings for the abbreviated forms of this character. Here we add a primitive meaning for the full character, one that should be easy to associate: **Eiffel Tower.** [10]	

1606		ointment
膏	*Eiffel Tower . . . flesh.* Note how the topmost primitive here is condensed to make room for the primitive under it. [14]	
	髙　膏	

1607	go smoothly

亨

Tall . . . -ed. These primitives present something of a challenge. Begin with a situation that comes to mind when you hear the key word, **go smoothly**. Say, an interview. Your friend, a 7-foot-*tall* high-school basketball star, is being interviewed for entrance into an Ivy League school where he hopes to pursue a career in nuclear medicine, despite academic grades in the lower half of the alphabet. When he comes out, you ask him, "How'd it go?" To which he replies, "Duh. I tink it **go**-*ed* **smoothly**." [7]

亠　亨

1608	hum [v.]

哼

Mouth . . . go smoothly. [10]

口　哼

1609	honest

淳

Water . . . enjoy. [11]

氵　淳

1610	whale

鯨

The **whale** swallows a whole school of *fish*, who turn their new abode into a proper little *fish-capital*. [19]

魚　鯨

1611	redeem

贖

Shells . . . sell. [22]

貝　贖

LESSON 15

1612	**daylight**
晝	*Brush . . . daybreak.* [11]
	書 晝

1613	**Tianjin**
津	*Water . . . brush.* This character serves as an abbreviation for the important Chinese city of **Tianjin**. [9]
	氵 津

1614	**smidgen**
釐	*Not yet . . . taskmaster . . . cliff . . . computer.* [18]
	未 敉 斄 釐

1615	**small objects·**
枚	The key word has been chosen to represent the character's use as a "measure word" for counting coins, paper clips, cuff links, and the like. The elements are: *tree . . . taskmaster.* [8]
	木 枚

1616	**herd** (v.)
牧	Rather than go through the time and expense of training dogs to **herd** the *cows* back into the barn at night, we appoint one of the elder *cows* as *taskmaster*, fitting her out with a gown, spectacles, and a whip. [8]
	牛 牧

1617		rose

玫 *Jewel . . . taskmaster.* [8]

王　玫

1618		candid

敦 *Enjoy . . . taskmaster.* [12]

享　敦

❖	{212}	Disneyland

若 It is a short leap from the key-word meaning, *as if,* to the magical world of make-believe, **Disneyland.** [9]

1619		promise [N.]

諾 *Words . . . Disneyland.* [16]

言　諾

1620		meaning

謂 *Words . . . stomach.* [16]

言　謂

1621		inquire

詢 *Words . . . decameron.* [13]

言　詢

1622		penalize

罰 *Net . . . words . . . saber.* [14]

罒　罰　罰

1623	place an order
訂	*Words . . . nail.* Think of the *words* you use to *nail* down your choices as you **place an order** with the waiter. [9]

言 訂

1624	chant [v.]
詠	Listening to the *words* of monks as they **chant** their sutras is like being transported for a moment into *eternity*, where the rules of everyday life have been suspended. [12]

言 詠

1625	espionage
諜	*Words . . . family tree.* [16]

言 諜

1626	annotate
註	*Words . . . candlestick.* [12]

言 註

1627	forgive
諒	*Words . . . capitol building.* [15]

言 諒

1628	praise [v.]
讚	*Words . . . lifesaver.* [26]

言 讚

LESSON 16

1629

II

貳

The use of the Roman numeral **II** is intended to help capture the sense of a "fraud-proof" writing of the Chinese numeral for "2" in official documents. The primitive elements are: *arrow . . . two . . . shell.* [12]

一　三　貢　貳

1630

sick and tired of

膩

Flesh . . . II. [16]

月　膩

1631

discharge [v.]

洩

You will need to take a moment with this unfamiliar shape. The *water* on the left is clear. Next draw the *sun*. Finally, draw a broken *halberd,* a mere stick without the blade at the top (the final stroke of *halberd*), noting how the third stroke of *sun* and the first of *halberd* double up.

The character is not as difficult to remember as it might look at first sight. Imagine someone with a musket that shoots *halberds* instead of bullets—a cross between a bazooka and a harpoon thrower. Suffering from dehydration our musketeer turns angry at the gods and, as the ancient Gauls did when they lost a battle and shot arrows at the sky to complain, **discharges** a barrage of *halberds* at the *sun* while crying out, "*Water, water!*" [9]

氵　沪　洩

1632

paddle [v.]

划

Fiesta . . . saber. The key word refers to what we do with oars, not with what old-style pedagogues used to do to misbehaving children. [6]

戈 划

1633 caw (N.)

嗄

The **caw** sound is considered a bad omen. Take advantage of this when making your story. *Mouth . . . ceiling . . . nostrils . . . fiesta.* [14]

口　口￣　咟　嗄

1634 domain

域

If you think of an Internet **domain**, you will not be far from the connotation of this word, which refers to an area of control. The elements are: *land . . . or.* [11]

圡　域

1635 sow (V.)

栽

One way of celebrating *Thanksgiving* is to do something that others will remember at a future *Thanksgiving* dinner—like going out to the garden to **sow** the seeds for a row of cranberry *trees.* [10]

圡　耒　栽

1636 kin

戚

Parade . . . above . . . small. [11]

一　厂　厈　厈　戚

1637 despise

蔑

Flowers . . . net . . . march. Note that because there is nothing actually *marching* under the enclosure for *march*, the horizontal stroke is dropped downward to fill in the space. It is only a matter of aesthetics, so you should not let it bother you too much. [15]

艹　茜　蔑

1638		yell (v.)
喊	Mouth . . . everybody. [12]	
	口　喊	

1639		splatter (v.)
濺	Water . . . cheap. [18]	
	氵　濺	

LESSON 17

1640	address [N.]
址	Soil . . . footprint. [7]
	土　址

1641	astringent
澀	Water . . . two blades . . . two footprints. [17]
	氵　氵　氵　澀　澀

1642	apple
蘋	Flowers . . . repeatedly. [20]
	艹　蘋

1643	go to
赴	When you **go to** a new job in a new city, something in you wants to *walk* ahead confidently with enthusiastic strides. But then something else in you wants you to hold back, like a *divining rod* built into your psyche warning you about rushing in too carelessly. [9]
	走　赴

1644	trip
趟	This is not an actual **trip** but a "measure word" or "classifier" for **trips** taken. Treat this and other classifiers as nouns when you make your stories. Its elements: *walk* . . . *esteem*. [15]
	走　趟

1645	dike

堤

A **dike** is *soil* piled up in advance of a disaster. There is no way of predicting if the great inundation is to **be** or not to **be**, but in either case, the town will be ready. [12]

土　堤

1646	keyboard keys

鍵

Metal . . . build. [17]

金　鍏　鍵

1647	son-in-law

婿

What turns a bachelor into a **son-in-law** (or at least used to) is a *woman* and her dowry, here presented as a small *zoo* (since animals were often used for the purpose in earlier societies) and a *month* away from it all (the "honey*moon*"). [12]

女　妬　婿

LESSON 18

THE TIME has come to roll up your sleeves. Unlike the previous lessons, which were relatively short, many of the following lessons will be considerably longer. In this one you will learn 42 new characters.

1648	tailor [v.]
裁	*Thanksgiving . . . clothing.* [12]

土　表　裁

1649	socks
襪	*Cloak . . . despise* [20]

衤　襪

1650	trundle [v.]
滚	*Water . . . six . . . mouth . . . scarf.* If it's any help, this is one of the Chinese characters that figures in the compound word for rock 'n' roll (or more accurately, "oscillate 'n' **trundle**"). [14]

氵　氵　滂　滚

1651	decline [v.]
衰	Refer back to FRAME 377 and the character meaning *grief.* The story recalls the colorful actor, W. C. Fields. It is a little known fact, but as he grew older and began to **decline,** his trademark smirk also started to droop. Plastic surgery being still in its covered wagon days, he had no choice but insert a *walking stick* into his cheeks sideways, and thus maintain his image. [10]

亠　亡　亡　亡　衰

1652	innermost feelings

衷

Following on the story from the previous frame, let's say the short, vertical *walking stick* here is not for supporting one's outer frame but one's **innermost feelings**. In the case of W. C. Fields, it sustained the actor's awareness of the *grief* his fictitious alcoholism was causing those around him. [10]

亠　亠　声　衷

1653	meditation

禪

This is the character for Chinese **Chan** (or Zen). Its elements are: *altar . . . list*. [16]

礻　禪

1654	ape

猿

The suspicious politician *Yuan* first encountered in FRAME 378 OF Book 1 is depicted here as an **ape** being hounded by a *pack of wild dogs*, obviously from the opposition party. [13]

犭　猿

1655	dangle

吊

Mouth . . . towel. [6]

口　吊

1656	handkerchief

帕

Towel . . . white. Compare this character to the primitive element for *white towel* we met in Book 1 (page 164). [8]

巾　帕

1657	note (N.)
帖	*Towel . . . tell fortunes.* The key word refers to a memo you leave for someone, not musical annotation. [8]

巾　帖

1658	sail (N.)
帆	*Towel . . . ordinary.* [6]

巾　帆

1659	width of cloth
幅	*Towel . . . wealth.* [12]

巾　幅

1660	brocade
錦	*Gold . . . white towel.* [16]

金　錦

1661	copious
沛	*Water . . . market.* [8]

氵　沛

1662	persimmon
柿	*Tree . . . market.* [9]

木　柿

1663	stir up trouble
鬧	*Fight . . . market.* [15]

鬥 鬧

| 1664 | thorn bushes |

棘

Thorns alongside *thorns*. [12]

束 棘

| 1665 | jujube |

棗

Thorns on top of *thorns*. A **jujube** is a kind of Chinese date sometimes used in traditional medicine for sore throats. [12]

束 棗

| 1666 | flower bud |

蕾

Flowers . . . thunder. [17]

艹 蕾

| 1667 | gulp down |

吞

Die young . . . mouth. [7]

夭 吞

| 1668 | bewitching |

妖

Woman . . . die young. [7]

女 妖

| 1669 | fertile |

沃

Water . . . die young. Think of this key word as having to do with productive soil. [7]

氵 沃

1670	sedan chair
轎	Traditionally in China, the bride had to leave her family home and go to the groom's home on the wedding day. The bride would sit on a special kind of *cart* known as a **sedan chair,** as the groom and his relatives carried her to her new abode. The *angel* here is, of course, the bride. [19]

車　轎

1671	garbage
垃	*Soil . . . vase.* [8]

土　垃

1672	weep aloud
啼	*Mouth . . . sovereign.* [12]

口　啼

1673	fruit stem
蒂	*Flowers . . . sovereign.* [13]

艹　蒂

1674	drip (v.)
滴	*Water . . . antique.* [14]

氵　滴

1675	100 Chinese acres
頃	You may want to consult FRAME 779 of Book 1 to have a look at the character that means a single *Chinese acre.* The elements here: *spoon . . . head.* [11]

匕　頃

1676	spoon (N.)
匙	Be . . . ancient spoon. [11]

是　匙

1677	well-behaved
乖	Thousand . . . north. [8]

千　乖　乖

❖ For the primitive meaning, think of a particular *goody-goody* from your school days, always ready to please the teachers and the butt of everyone's jokes.

1678	hitch a ride
乘	Goody-goody . . . umbrella. Note how the last two strokes, which we have given as the element for *umbrella,* are drawn the same as the final two strokes in the character for "tree." [10]

乖　乖　乘

1679	leftover (ADJ.)
剩	Try associating this key word with the **leftover** grub in your refrigerator. Its elements: *hitch a ride . . . saber.* [12]

乘　剩

1680	club (N.)
棍	The **club** depicted in this character is a throwback to the time when discipline was meted out by beating people silly. Here the **club** is an entire *tree* wielded by a tyrannical patriarch on his *descendants* for not eating their Brussels sprouts. [12]

木　棍

1681	in accord

諧

Words . . . all-temperature detergent (see FRAME 425). As the "chord" in **accord** suggests, the key word connotes things in harmony. [16]

言　諧

1682	firewood

柴

This (literary) . . . tree. [10]

此　柴

1683	quick-witted

敏

Every taskmaster worth his salt needs a repertoire of **quick-witted** retorts. For example, "The last thing I want to do is hurt you. But it's still on my list." [11]

每　敏

1684	mildew (N.)

霉

Weather . . . every. [15]

雨　霉

1685	so far

迄

The key word indicates the extent of something in a temporal or spatial sense, but for your story stick with the temporal sense of something that hasn't happened **so far**. *Beg . . . road.* [6]

乞　迄

1686	chop (V.)

砍

Stone . . . yawn. Keep distinct from the primitive for *chop* learned in Book 1. [9]

石　砍

1687

坎　　　　　　　　　　　　　　　　　　　　　　hump [N.]

Soil . . . yawn/lack. When you speak of "getting over the **hump**," you mean getting yourself past the bumpiest and most difficult stage of something or making it past the halfway point. As with an illness, a final exam, or the cold of winter. [7]

土　坎

1688

炊　　　　　　　　　　　　　　　　　　　　　　cook [V.]

Picture what happens to people who try to **cook** their supper when they should be taking a nap after a hard day's work. Here we see a *fire* blazing out of control as a hapless young executive *yawns* inattentively. [8]

火　炊

1689

欽　　　　　　　　　　　　　　　　　think highly of

Metal . . . yawn. [12]

金　欽

LESSON 19

BEGINNING with this lesson, we will be introducing completely new primitive elements not based on characters already learned. Their component parts will all be elements learned in this or a previous lesson.

1690		cut open
剖	*Muzzle . . . saber.* [10]	
	音　剖	

1691		bodhisattva
菩	*Flowers . . . muzzle.* [12]	
	艹　菩	

1692		mango
芒	*Flowers . . . perish.* [7]	
	艹　芒	

1693		wasteland
荒	*Mango . . . flood.* [10]	
	艹　荒	

1694		lie (N.)
謊	*Words . . . wasteland.* [17]	
	言　謊	

1695   **boundless**

茫

Mango . . . water. Note how the *water* element snuggles in next to the element for *perish* rather than stand alone on the left as we might expect it to. [10]

艹   氵   茫

1696   **win** [v.]

贏

Perish . . . mouth . . . flesh . . . oyster . . . ordinary. [20]

亡   言   肓   贏   贏

❖   **crochet needles**

卂

The *hook* and the *needle* easily suggest the little basket of **crochet needles** (or *hooks*) your grandmother kept next to her rocking chair, where she sat quietly whipping you up a fancy muffler. [3]

乁   卂

1697   **interrogate**

訊

Words . . . crochet needles. [10]

言   訊

1698   **workshop**

坊

Soil . . . compass. [7]

土   坊

1699   **aromatic**

芳

Here we see a special *compass* used to pick out those *flowers* most suited for making **aromatic** perfumes. It was originally invented by a bee that had no sense of direction. [8]

艹 芳

1700

call on

訪

When you have to **call on** a dignitary, you have to frame your *words* with great care. Hence the need for a grammatical *compass*. [6]

言　訪

1701

stew (v.)

熬

Soil . . . release . . . cooking fire. Note how the left half of *release* has to be pressed down in order to squeeze into the space under *soil*. [15]

土　敖　熬

1702

tobacco

菸

Flowers . . . (all-purpose preposition). [12]

艹　菸

❖　{466}

Magellan

旁

The adventurer Ferdinand **Magellan** is remembered for having been the first person to sail around the world, but scholars of history have forgotten his little-known *side*kick, Pacifica, after whom he would name an entire ocean. [10]

亠　产　旁

1703

roster

榜

Tree . . . Magellan. [12]

扌　榜

1704	pound [N.]
磅	You have heard of the Rosetta Stone, the ancient Egyptian key to unlocking hieroglyphic writing. Here we have the less known, and, truth be told, historically suspect, *Magellan stone*, which was used to figure out just how much a **pound** really weighed in ancient times. [15]

石　磅

1705	upper arm
膀	*Flesh . . . Magellan.* [14]

月　膀

1706	sharp
銳	*Metal . . . devil.* [15]

金　銳

Lesson 20

1707	rainbow
虹	*Insect . . . I-beam.* [9]
	虫　虹

1708	bat (N.)
蝠	The **bat** this character refers to is the flying rodent that hangs around bell towers and damp caves. Its elements: *insect . . . wealth.* [15]
	虫　蝠

1709	frog
蛙	*Insect . . . bricks.* [12]
	虫　蛙

1710	locust
蝗	*Insect . . . emperor.* [15]
	虫　蝗

1711	cicada
蟬	*Insect . . . list.* [18]
	虫　蟬

1712	maple
楓	*Tree . . . windstorm.* [13]
	木　楓

1713		placenta
胞	*Part of the body . . . wrap.* [9]	
	月 胞	

1714		fireworks
炮	*Fire . . . wrap.* [9]	
	火 炮	

1715		robe (N.)
袍	*Cloak . . . wrap.* [10]	
	衤 袍	

1716		hail
雹	*Rain . . . wrap.* [13]	
	雨 雹	

1717		pursue
逐	*Sow . . . road.* [10]	
	豕 逐	

1718		satisfy
遂	*Animal horns . . . pursue.* [12]	
	ⸯ 遂	

1719		Mongolia
蒙	As with Los Angeles and England (FRAMES 286 and 1278), this frame shows us the first character in the fuller compound for the proper noun. Its component primitives: *flowers . . . crown . . . ceiling . . . sow.* [14]	

艹　芦　芦　蒙

1720　　　　　　　　　　　　　　　　　　　　dim ^(ADJ.)

朦　　*Moon . . . Mongolia.* [18]

月　朦

1721　　　　　　　　　　　　　　　　　　　unrestrained

豪　　*Tiara . . . sow.* [14]

亠　豪

❖

豕　　The short stroke in the legs of the *sow* gives us the primitive element meaning **hog-tied**. [8]

豸　豸　豕

1722　　　　　　　　　　　　　　　　　　　　peck ^(v.)

啄　　*Mouth . . . hog-tied.* [11]

口　啄

1723　　　　　　　　　　　　　　　　　　　chisel ^(v.)

琢　　*King . . . hog-tied.* [12]

王　琢

1724　　　　　　　　　　　　　　　　　　　　marry

嫁　　The primitive on the left makes it clear that this is a character depicting a *woman* who **marries** and moves with her spouse into a new home—in this case, a *flophouse* (an alternative primitive meaning for the character *house*). [13]

女　嫁

1725	intestines
腸	*Part of the body . . . piggy bank.* [13]

月　腸

1726	poplar
楊	*Tree . . . piggy bank.* [13]

扌　楊

1727	scald
燙	During lunch break in the chemistry lab, you are boiling your *soup* in a bowl that you are holding over the large single flame (the full character for *fire*) of a Bunsen burner. Having not yet mastered the basic principles of chemistry, you learn lesson no. 1 the hard way: the bowl, too, gets hot! You drop it on your lap and learn lesson no. 2: hot *soup* **scalds**. [16]

湯　燙

1728	licentious
蕩	*Flowers . . . soup.* [16]

艹　蕩

1729	detailed
詳	*Words . . . sheep.* [13]

言　詳

1730	envy (v.)
羨	*Sheep . . . water . . . yawn/lack.* Although this character looks rather simple, special care should be taken in learning it because of the proximity of the final two elements to the character for *next*. Note, too, that the *water* comes UNDER the *sheep*, rather than on its own to the left. [13]

羊 芏 羡

1731		solely
唯	Mouth . . . turkey. [11]	
	口　唯	

1732		pile (N./V.)
堆	Soil . . . turkey. [11]	
	土　堆	

1733		apprehensive
焦	Turkey . . . cooking fire. [12]	
	隹　焦	

❖ When used as a primitive element, this character will mean pretty much what it looks like: a *roast turkey*.

1734		lay eyes on
瞧	Eyeballs . . . roast turkey. [17]	
	目　瞧	

1735		reef
礁	Stone . . . roast turkey. [17]	
	石　礁	

1736		banana
蕉	Flower . . . roast turkey. [16]	
	艹　蕉	

1737		sculpture
雕	Circumference . . . turkey. [16]	

周　雕

1738		lop off
截	Thanksgiving . . . turkey. [14]	

土　隹　截

1739		allow
准	Ice . . . turkey. [10]	

冫　准

1740		sparrow
雀	Few . . . turkey. Note how the final stroke of *few* is elongated to double up as the first stroke of *turkey*. [11]	

少　雀

1741		all at once
霍	Suddenly, unexpectedly, the week before Thanksgiving it happened: **All at once** a *rain* of *turkeys* fell from the skies, causing havoc in the automobile insurance industry. [16]	

雨　霍

❖		St. Gobbler
奞	This character shows us a kind of chimera that came from a loony scientist splicing genes: the head is a *St. Bernard dog* and the back end is a *turkey*. Since no one has yet named the critter, we shall—the **St. Gobbler**. The only question is whether to cook it or teach it tricks.	

This primitive is always written ATOP another primitive. [11]

六 奮

1742　　　　　　　　　　　　　　　　　exert oneself

奮　　*St. Gobbler . . . rice field.* [16]

奞　奮

1743　　　　　　　　　　　　　　　　　take by force

奪　Whereas *burglars* (FRAME 337) appropriate another's property clandestinely, robbers and muggers prefer to confront their victims and **take by force** what is not theirs. The primitive elements: *St. Gobbler. . . glued to.* [14]

奞　奪

1744　　　　　　　　　　　　　　　　　turn upward

翹　This key word is meant to connote the way things like hair, eyelashes, and puppy dog tails **turn upward**. The elements are: *Pigpen . . . wings.* [18]

堯　翹

1745　　　　　　　　　　　　　　　　　fall down

塌　The key word can be used for all sorts of things that **fall down**, from rooftops to hairdos. The primitive elements: *soil . . . sun . . . wings.* [13]

士　坍　塌

1746　　　　　　　　　　　　　　　　　writing brush

翰　*Mist . . . umbrella . . . wings.* [16]

卓　斡　翰

LESSON 21

As MENTIONED in Lesson 21 of Book 1, from this point on the stroke order will not be given unless it is entirely new, departs from the procedures we have learned so far, or might otherwise cause confusion.

❖ 囷	{518}	**dog kennel**
	The *pent-in St. Bernard dog* makes the primitive meaning of a **dog kennel** a natural selection. [6]	
1747 咽		**throat**
	Mouth . . . dog kennel. [9]	
1748 姻		**in-law** (ADJ.)
	Woman . . . dog kennel. [9]	
1749 廟		**temple**
	Cave . . . dynasty. Be sure to keep this character distinct from that for a *Buddhist temple* (FRAME 155). [15]	
1750 廂		**side room**
	Cave . . . one another. [12]	
1751 嘛		**(pause marker)**
	This is a particle that is used within a sentence to mark a pause, drawing attention to what will follow. Its elements: *mouth . . . hemp.* [14]	
1752 磨		**grind** (V.)
	Hemp . . . stone. [16]	
1753 廈		**skyscraper**
	Cave . . . summer. [13]	

1754 廁	toilet
	Cave . . . rule. [12]

1755 悟	realize
	State of mind . . . I (literary). As the primitives indicate, this has to do with coming to awareness, not with getting a return on one's investments. [10]

1756 忠	loyal
	Middle . . . heart. [8]

1757 悼	mourn
	State of mind . . . eminent. [11]

1758 慎	prudent
	State of mind . . . true. [13]

1759 恕	pardon (v.)
	Be like . . . heart. [10]

1760 悄	noiseless
	State of mind . . . candle. [10]

1761 恍	all of a sudden
	State of mind . . . ray. [9]

1762 惰	indolent
	State of mind . . . left . . . flesh. You have seen the combination on the right once (FRAME 985) and you will meet it again (FRAME 2271). If you want to make a primitive element out of it, be our guest. [12]

1763 恢	immense
	State of mind . . . ashes. [9]

1764 恒	**permanent** *State of mind . . . sunrise, sunset.* Note that this primitive is taken from the explanation in FRAME 184, and has not been used since then. [9]
1765 慕	**admire** *Graveyard . . . valentine.* [15]
1766 恰	**just right** *State of mind . . . fit.* [9]
1767 惶	**fearful** *State of mind . . . emperor.* [12]
1768 愉	**overjoyed** The daily joy of the *slaughterhouse* is to be delivered a fresh load of beef on the hoof. But here the butchers are in an **overjoyed** *state of mind*, presumably because Jurassic Park has closed down and they get first rights to the exotic livestock. [12]
1769 愈	**more and more** *Slaughterhouse . . . heart.* [13]
1770 惑	**be bewildered** *Or . . . heart.* [12]
1771 怔	**terror-stricken** *State of mind . . . correct.* [8]
1772 怖	**be scared of** *State of mind . . . cloth.* [8]
1773 添	**augment** *Water . . . die young . . . valentine.* [11]

1774 悔	be sorry about
State of mind . . . every. [10]	

1775 慌	nervous
State of mind . . . wasteland [13]	

1776 悦	delighted
State of mind . . . devil. [10]	

1777 憎	loathe
State of mind . . . increase. [15]	

1778 忌	shun
Snake . . . heart. [7]	

1779 惟	thinking
State of mind . . . turkey. [11]	

1780 懼	be frightened
State of mind . . . two eyeballs . . . turkey. [21]	

1781 患	troubles
String together . . . heart. [11]	

1782 惹	provoke
Disneyland . . . heart. [13]	

1783 恩	kindness
Dog kennel . . . heart. [10]	

1784 憶	recall (v.)
State of mind . . . idea. [16]	

1785 媳	daughter-in-law
	Woman . . . breath. [13]

1786 熄	put out
	Since this character is used to **put out** lights and fires (but not the cat), its elements remind us of what we do to the candles on a birthday cake: *fire . . . breath.* [14]

1787 瑟	Chinese harp
	Two *balls . . . certainly.* [13]

1788 泌	secrete
	Water . . . certainly. [8]

1789 蜜	honey
	House . . . certainly . . . insect. [14]

LESSON 22

THE 88 CHARACTERS of this lesson make it the longest of the book. The elements introduced in Book 1 at this point leave us no choice. In any case, you will want to break it up into two or three study sessions.

1790		rub [v.]
摩	*Hemp . . . hand.* [15]	
❖	{551}	miser
我	In place of the key-word meaning, *I*, we will assign this character the primitive meaning of an *I*-centered individual, the **miser.** [7]	
1791		moth
蛾	*Insect . . . miser.* [13]	
1792		pick pockets [v.]
扒	*Fingers . . . eight.* [5]	
1793		button [N./V.]
扣	*Fingers . . . mouth.* [6]	
1794		contribute
捐	*Fingers . . . mouth . . . flesh.* [10]	
1795		racquet
拍	*Fingers . . . dove/white.* [8]	
1796		clapping sound
啪	The sound a rifle makes or the applause of an audience are both covered by this key word, **clapping sound.** The elements are: *mouth . . . racquet* [11]	

1797	damage [v.]
損	*Fingers . . . employee.* [13]

1798	carry over the shoulder
扛	*Fingers . . . I-beam.* [6]

1799	prick [v.]
扎	*Fingers . . . fishhook.* [4]

1800	thumb
拇	*Fingers . . . mother.* [8]

1801	detain
拘	*Fingers . . . sentence.* [8]

1802	copy [v.]
抄	*Fingers . . . few.* Anything one **copies** by hand is covered by this character; copying things by machine is not. [7]

1803	pioneer [v.]
拓	This key word can refer to opening up new territory in both the geographical and figurative senses. *Fingers . . . rocks.* [8]

1804	pinch [v.]
捏	*Fingers . . . sun . . . soil.* [10]

1805	chafe
撓	*Fingers . . . Pigpen.* The sense of the key word is to scratch or abrade. [15]

1806	smear on
抹	*Fingers . . . last.* For the sense of this key word, think of when you **smear on** sunscreen lotion. [8]

1807 描	describe *Fingers . . . tomato seedling.* [12]
1808 摸	grope *Fingers . . . graveyard.* The primitives nicely suggest "to **grope** around in the dark." [14]
1809 挑	foment *Fingers . . . portent.* [9]
1810 拴	tether (v.) *Fingers . . . whole.* [9]
1811 拾	tidy up *Fingers . . . fit.* [9]
1812 搭	put up The key word means to **put up** a structure, like a tent or a small shed. Its elements are: *finger . . . flowers . . . fit.* You may recall that we already met the combination of elements on the right in FRAME 247 of Book 1. [13]
1813 掠	pillage (v.) *Fingers . . . capital.* [11]
1814 捨	abandon *Fingers . . . abode.* [11]
1815 拭	wipe away *Fingers . . . style.* [9]
1816 扯	yank (v.) *Fingers . . . footprint.* [7]

1817	drag (v.)
拖	*Fingers . . . reclining . . . scorpion.* Take care to create an image for this key word that does not conflict with the one you used for the primitive element of the same meaning. [8]

1818	publicize
揚	*Fingers . . . piggy bank.* [12]

1819	engage in
搞	*Fingers . . . Eiffel Tower.* [13]

1820	bump into
撞	Think of billiard balls that you persuade with a cue stick to **bump into** each other on a pool table. Only—to your utter surprise—you find that the balls exchange greetings as they **bump into** each other. "Hello, long time no see. How ya doin' there, 9-ball?" If you can picture a *juvenile* forming a bridge with his *fingers* to guide the cue stick to the cue ball, you should have no trouble with this one. [15]

1821	handpick
摘	*Fingers . . . antique.* The sense of this key word is to gather or pick by hand, not the more figurative sense to single out for special treatment. [14]

1822	lash together
捆	*Fingers . . . trapped.* In case you had any doubts, this character does not refer to engaging in communal flagellation but to the binding of things into a bundle. [10]

1823	joggle (v.)
撼	*Fingers . . . feel.* [16]

1824	harass
擾	*Fingers . . . worried.* [18]

	Mr. Hyde
❖ 亶	The *top hat* that *returns* at *daybreak* is none other than **Mr. Hyde** *returning* to his daytime identity as Dr. Jekyll. [13]

亠　　回　　亶

1825	act without authority
擅	*Fingers . . . Mr. Hyde.* [16]

1826	altar
壇	Here we have the full character for an **altar**, not to be confused with the image you used for the primitive element of the same name. Its elements: *soil . . . Mr. Hyde.* [16]

1827	tremble
顫	*Mr. Hyde . . . head.* [22]

1828	rude
莽	*Flowers . . . chihuahua . . . two hands.* [11]

1829	take precautions against
戒	The *two hands* being waved about furiously in a *fiesta* belong to the security guards who are advising people to **take precautions against** getting run over by the floats or getting knocked on the head by a butterfingered twirler's baton. [7]

1830	weapon
械	*Tree . . . take precautions against.* [11]

1831	warn
誡	*Words . . . take precautions against.* [14]

❖

卉

haystack

The *two hands* here are fumbling around in the **haystack** looking for a *needle*. (Or, if you prefer to see the primitive as a drawing of three *needles*, you end up having to look for the **haystack** in the *needles*. Now that's a switch!) [5]

十　卉

1832

奔

dash (v.)

St. Bernard dog . . . haystack. [8]

❖

賁

local-yokel chowder

Living too far from the ocean to rely on a steady supply of *clams*, the local yokels of Hayseed County have invented something they like to call "*clam* helper." Take two small stacks of premium-quality *hay*, add two bushels of fresh spuds, and a dash of salt to taste. Boil in a hogshead cask for four hours or until the hay is completely dissolved. Take this "*clam*-helper" mix and pour into a bowl with a single frozen *clam* at the bottom. Voilà—le **local-yokel chowder**. Serves one. [12]

卉　賁

1833

噴

spurt (v.)

Mouth . . . local-yokel chowder. [15]

1834

墳

tomb

Soil . . . local-yokel chowder. [15]

1835

憤

indignation

State of mind . . . local-yokel chowder. [15]

1836

材

stuff (N.)

This character is used for materials for teaching, construction, and all sorts of other things. Its elements: *tree . . . genie.* [7]

1837 孕	pregnant *Only then/fist . . . child.* [5]
1838 扔	throw away *Fingers . . . fist.* [5]
1839 圾	trash ^(N.) *Soil . . . outstretched hands.* [6]
1840 叉	fork ^(N.) *Crotch/right hand . . . drop of.* [3]
1841 桑	mulberry tree Three *crotches . . . tree.* [10]
1842 嗓	voicebox *Mouth . . . mulberry tree.* [13]
1843 寇	outlaw ^(N.) The final stroke of the character for *finish* (the first seven strokes) wraps itself around the primitives for *magic wand* and *crotch* to give us the character for **outlaw**. [11]
1844 敲	knock ^(V.) *Eiffel Tower . . . magic wand . . . crotch.* [14]
1845 灌	pour into *Water . . . stork.* [21]
1846 權	authority *Tree . . . stork.* [22]

1847	resolute
毅	*Standing up . . . sow . . . missile.* The final stroke of *standing up* doubles up with the first stroke of *sow.* [15]

1848	limb
肢	*Flesh . . . branch.* With *flesh* as a component of the character, it should be clear that this key word refers to a **limb** of a body, of course, not of a tree. [8]

1849	prostitute
妓	*Woman . . . branch.* [7]

1850	fork in the road
歧	*Footprints . . . branch.* [8]

1851	fins
翅	*Branch . . . wings.* [10]

1852	graceful
淑	*Water . . . uncle.* This character is generally reserved for women and women's names. [11]

1853	spice plant
椒	*Tree . . . uncle.* [12]

1854	queen
后	*Drag . . . ceiling . . . mouth.* [6]

1855	shield (N.)
盾	*Drag . . . ten . . . eyeballs.* [9]

1856	peddler
販	*Shells . . . against.* [11]

1857 扳 *Fingers . . . against.* [7]	tug [(v.)]
1858 覓 *Vulture . . . see.* [11]	try to find
1859 妥 *Vulture . . . woman.* [7]	appropriate [(ADJ.)]
1860 睬 *Eyeball . . . pluck.* [13]	notice [(v.)]
1861 允 The card affirming that you **consent** to have your body parts harvested in case of sudden death usually refers to organs, but this fellow—obviously a professional basketball player at the peak of his career—stipulates that only his *elbows* and *human legs* are to be donated to science. [4]	consent [(v.)]
1862 勾 *Bound up . . . elbow.* [4]	cross out
1863 晉 *Ceiling . . . two elbows . . . floor . . . sun.* [10]	promote
1864 宏 *House . . . by one's side . . . elbow.* [7]	magnificent
1865 胎 *Part of the body . . . platform.* [9]	fetus
1866 冶 *Ice . . . platform.* [7]	smelt [(v.)]

1867	typhoon
颱	*Windstorm . . . platform.* Note how the final stroke of *windstorm* "encloses" the element for *platform* from the bottom. [14]

1868	negligent
怠	*Platform . . . heart.* [9]

1869	elevate
抬	*Fingers . . . platform.* [8]

1870	mislay
丢	*Thousand . . . walls.* [6]

1871	Taiwan
臺	*Aerosol can . . . crown . . . until.* This is the first character in the traditional compound for **Taiwan**. (The second, if you don't already know it, can be found in FRAME 1024 of Book 1.) [14]

1872	bring about
致	*Until . . . taskmaster.* The sense of the key word is to cause something to happen. [10]

1873	remove
撤	*Fingers . . . education . . . taskmaster.* [15]

1874	sulfur
硫	*Stone . . . baby Moses.* [12]

1875	glaze (N.)
琉	*King . . . baby Moses.* [11]

1876	sparse
疏	*Zoo . . . baby Moses.* You will note that the primitive for *zoo* looks slightly different from the form you learned in Book 1

(疋). In order to fit it on the left, the strokes have to be cramped together, as shown below. [12]

⁷　　了　　禾　　疋　　疋　　疏

1877　　　　　　　　　　　　　　　　　　　　**veggies**

蔬

The key word refers to vegetables, but should be kept distinct from the character of that name (FRAME 666). Its primitives: *flowers . . . sparse.* [16]

LESSON 23

1878 崩	**crumble** *Mountain . . . companion.* The key word has to do with the collapse of large structures, not with what happens to cookies or bread. [11]
1879 岩	**rock** *Mountain . . . stone.* [8]
1880 崎	**rugged** *Mountain . . . strange.* The key word refers to the terrain, not to a character trait. [11]
1881 崖	**cliff** *Mountain . . . cliff . . . bricks.* This is the full character from which we derived the primitive element of the same name. [11]
1882 炭	**charcoal** *Mountain . . . ashes.* [9]
1883 碳	**carbon** *Stone . . . charcoal.* [14]
1884 盼	**await hopefully** *Eyeball . . . part.* [9]
1885 頒	**promulgate** *Part . . . head.* [13]

1886 芬	essence *Flowers . . . part.* The meaning of this key word has nothing to do with the goal of a phenomenological reduction, but with the sweet-smelling fragrance of plants and herbs extracted in order to disguise the olfactory truth. [8]
1887 扮	play the part of *Fingers . . . part.* [7]
1888 岔	diverge *Part . . . mountain.* [7]
1889 頌	extol *Public . . . head.* [13]
1890 訟	litigate *Words . . . public.* [11]
1891 翁	elderly man *Public . . . feathers.* [10]
1892 裕	abundant This character shows the typical *cloak* of *valley* folk, which, unlike the tailor-made, high-fashion overcoats of city folk, is loose fitting and free-form. Hence the key word's meaning of **abundant**. [12]
1893 榕	banyan *Tree . . . contain.* [14]

LESSON 24

1894 賞	prize *Outhouse . . . shells.* [15]
1895 嘗	attempt (v.) *Outhouse . . . purpose.* [14]
1896 嚐	taste (v.) *Mouth . . . attempt.* [17]
1897 掌	palm of the hand *Outhouse . . . hand.* [12]
1898 擋	fend off *Fingers . . . work as.* [16]
1899 膛	chest *Part of the body . . . main room.* [15]
1900 頗	quite *Covering . . . head.* [14]
1901 坡	slope (n.) *Soil . . . covering.* [8]
1902 披	drape over the shoulders *Fingers . . . covering.* [8]
1903 彼	the other Let this key word connote things like "**the other** person" or "**the other** part." Its elements: *queue . . . covering.* [8]

	hay bales
❖ 芻	The three strokes inside of the two elements for *bound up* are the old way of writing each side of the primitive for *flowers*. Although this does not apply to all **hay bales,** those made from alfalfa often have *flowers bound up* in them. Here we see two **hay bales** stacked atop one another. [10]

ノ　勹　勾　勾　芻　芻

1904		wrinkles
皺	*Hay bales . . . covering.* [15]	

1905		chick
雛	*Hay bales . . . turkey.* [18]	

1906		hasten
趨	*Walk . . . hay bales.* [17]	

1907		spinach
菠	*Flowers . . . waves.* [12]	

1908		breed (v.)
殖	*Bones . . . straight.* [12]	

1909		dissimilar
殊	*Bones . . . vermilion.* [10]	

1910		incomplete
殘	*Bones . . . float.* [12]	

1911		grin (v.)
咧	*Mouth . . . line up.* [9]	

1912 裂	crack (v.)
Line up . . . clothes. [12]	

1913 耿	dedicated
Ear . . . fire. [10]	

1914 恥	shame (n.)
Ear . . . heart. It is most rare to have the *heart* at the right, rather than at the bottom. Take advantage of this fact when you compose your story. [10]	

1915 輯	edit
Car . . . mouth . . . ear. [16]	

1916 攝	take a photo
Fingers . . . three ears. [21]	

1917 娶	take a wife
Take . . . woman. Compare this character for what a woman does when she marries into a family FRAME 1724. [11]	

1918 扶	lend a hand
Fingers . . . husband. [7]	

1919 熙	splendid
The first primitive looks like *underling*, except for the tiny little *mouth* in the middle—much as you would expect of a particularly fawning, bootlicking, toadying *underling* who responds to every suggestion of the boss with the exclamation, "**Splendid!**" without every venturing an opinion of his own. In this case, the boss has him roast a *snakeskin* belt and shoes over a *cooking fire* and eat them for supper. "**Splendid!**" the poor fellow exclaims as he takes his first bite. The drawing order is pretty much as you would expect, but we give it here to reinforce it all the same. [14]	

| 一 | 丁 | 厅 | 匝 | 臣 | 臣 | 臣 | 熙 |

1920 kidneys

腎 *Scrooge . . . part of the body.* [12]

1921 recruit (v.)

募 *Graveyard . . . muscle.* Note that the final stroke of *graveyard* has to be moved slightly to make enough room for what comes underneath. [13]

1922 threaten

脅 *Muscles* upon *muscles . . . flesh.* [10]

1923 inferior

劣 *Few . . . muscles.* [6]

1924 merit (N.)

勳 See if you can design in your head a scout **merit** badge acknowledging completion of the 42.195 kilometers of a marathon. Think of the trim and muscular physiques of great long-distance runners as you juggle the primitives in imagination: *a thousand black muscles.* [16]

1925 advise

勸 *Stork . . . muscle.* [20]

1926 plunder (v.)

劫 *Go . . . muscle.* [7]

1927 anger (N.)

怒 *Slave . . . heart.* [9]

1928 eggplant

茄 *Flowers . . . add.* [9]

1929 彷	seemingly
	Queue . . . compass. [7]

1930 征	go on an expedition
	Column . . . correct. [8]

1931 徒	follower
	Queue . . . walk. [10]

1932 徊	undecided
	Queue . . . return. [9]

1933 徵	solicit
	Queue . . . mountain . . . floor . . . jewel . . . taskmaster. [15]

1934 懲	chasten
	Solicit . . . heart. [19]

1935 循	comply with
	Queue . . . shield. [12]

1936 徹	thorough
	Queue . . . education . . . taskmaster. [15]

1937 役	service
	Queue . . . missile. This is the character used, for example, for military **service**. [7]

1938 衍	develop
	Boulevard . . . water. [9]

1939	weight
衡	To simplify what is located on the *boulevard*, think of a *St. Bernard dog* with a *fish* in its mouth, which accounts for the disappearance of the *fish's* "tail." [16]

1940	title
衒	*Boulevard . . . gold.* The **title** this character refers to is one having to do with rank or office. [14]

Lesson 25

1941 禿	bald
	Wild rice . . . human legs. [7]

1942 頹	decrepit
	Bald . . . head. [16]

1943 秒	seconds
	The reference here is to **seconds** of time, not to second helpings. The elements: *wild rice . . . few.* [9]

1944 稍	a little (ADV.)
	Wild rice . . . candle. The key word carries the sense of "slightly" or "to a small degree." [12]

1945 穌	rise again
	The sense of the key word is to revive or be restored to life. The elements are *fish . . . wild rice.* Note that in combination with the character for *Jerusalem* we will learn later (FRAME 2738), it transliterates the name of Jesus. [16]

1946 蘇	revive
	Flowers . . . rise again. The meaning of the key word is to regain consciousness or "come to." [20]

1947 萎	wilt
	Flowers . . . committee. [12]

❖ 黍	Rumpelbrella
	Rumpelstiltskin, you will recall, used a spinning wheel to turn straw into gold. Here we find his eccentric brother, **Rumpelbrella**, whose magical *umbrella* can turn *wild rice* into *snowflakes.* [12]

禾　夭　黍

1948 黏	sticky *Rumpelbrella . . . tell fortunes.* [17]
1949 黎	host^(N.) The key word has nothing to do with taking care of guests. It is a literary way of referring to masses of people. Take note of the placing of the elements: *Rumpelbrella . . . bound up . . . eyedropper.* [15]

禾　黎　黎

❖ 黍	Baron von Rumpelbrella Here we meet the unscrupulous uncle of *Rumpelbrella,* who managed to weasel out of his nephew the blueprints to the magical umbrella that turns wild rice into *snowflakes.* He adapted the technology to turn *trees* into *snowflakes* and amassed billions by "developing" the rain forest of the Amazon into a mega-resort for winter sports. **Baron von Rumpelbrella** and his entire empire are now under investigation by Interpol. [11]

木　夾　黍

1950 漆	wall paint *Water . . . Baron von Rumpelbrella.* [14]
1951 膝	knees *Flesh . . . Baron von Rumpelbrella.* [15]
1952 稠	dense *Wild rice . . . lap / circumference.* [13]

1953	draft (N.)
稿	The key word connotes the preliminary composition of a plan or manuscript. Its elements: *wild rice . . . Eiffel Tower*. [15]
1954	clever
穎	*Spoon . . . wild rice . . . head*. [16]
1955	tax (N.)
稅	*Wild rice . . . devil*. [12]
1956	crops
稼	*Wild rice . . . flophouse*. [15]
1957	fungus
菌	*Flowers . . . pent in . . . wild rice*. [12]
1958	immature
稚	*Wild rice . . . turkey*. [13]
1959	harvest (V.)
穫	*Wild rice . . . bird of paradise*. [19]
1960	private (ADJ.)
私	*Wild rice . . . elbow*. [7]
1961	order (N.)
秩	This key word has nothing to do with a command, but refers to a condition or state, as in the expression "in good **order**." The elements: *wild rice . . . lose*. [10]
1962	shell (N.)
殼	*Soldier . . . crown . . . one . . . wind . . . missile*. The **shell** of this character is different from the primitive element used for sea-shells. [12]

1963 穀	**cereal** Learn this character in connection with *shell* from the previous frame. The only difference is the substitution of *wild rice* in place of the *wind*. [15]
1964 鍬	**shovel** (N.) *Metal . . . autumn.* [17]
1965 揪	**hold tight** The sense of the key word is to grab hold of something firmly. The elements: *fingers . . . autumn.* [12]
1966 梨	**pear** *Profit . . . tree.* [11]
1967 犁	**plow** (N.) *Profit . . . cow.* [11]
1968 曆	**calendar** *Cliff . . .* two stalks of *standing grain . . . day.* [16]
1969 糕	**cake** *Rice . . . sheep . . . cooking fire.* [16]
1970 糊	**batter** **Batter** is usually made with great care to get just the right ingredients in just the right proportion, but *rice* **batter** (the source of the rarely served *rice* pancakes) is made by throwing all the ingredients into a large pot from across the room—the more *recklessly*, the better the **batter**. [15]
1971 粘	**glue** (V.) *Rice . . . tell fortunes.* Take care not to confuse with the primitive of the same meaning. [11]

1972 糧	provisions
	Rice . . . quantity. [18]

1973 菊	chrysanthemum
	Flower . . . bound up . . . rice. [12]

1974 糙	rough
	Rice . . . create. The key word refers to the texture of things, as of something **rough** to the touch. [16]

1975 粒	grain
	Rice . . . vase. As the primitive on the left suggests, **grain** here refers to granules, not to a pattern in wood. [11]

1976 燦	brilliant
	Fire . . . magic wand . . . evening . . . crotch . . . rice. [17]

1977 粉	powder
	Rice . . . part. [10]

1978 瞇	squint [v.]
	Eyeballs . . . lost. [14]

❖ 敝	shredder
	Ignoring for a moment the way this element is actually drawn, the left side looks like something with a *hood* that has *rice* coming out the top and bottom. Actually, those are just little pieces of paper spewing out in all directions from a document shredder. The familiar *taskmaster* standing off to the right gives the character its name. In his attempt to get just the right "look" to identify with his job, he ran his suit, shirt, and tie briefly through the **shredder**. [11]

` ˇ 肖 肖 肖 肖 敝

1979 幣	currency
	The key word **currency** refers here to money in circulation. Its elements: *shredder . . . towel.* [14]

1980 斃	die a violent death
	Shredder . . . death. [17]

1981 蔽	shelter [N.]
	Flowers . . . shredder. [15]

1982 撇	cast aside
	Fingers . . . shredder. [14]

1983 弊	fraud
	Shredder . . . two hands. [14]

1984 筍	bamboo shoot
	Bamboo . . . decameron. [12]

1985 筒	tube
	Bamboo . . . monks. [12]

1986 築	construct
	Bamboo . . . I-beam . . . ordinary . . . wood/tree. [16]

1987 笨	stupid
	Bamboo . . . notebook. [11]

1988 箭	arrow
	Bamboo . . . in front. In settling on a particular connotation for this key word, take care not to confuse it with the primitive for *arrow*, which does not appear in this character of the same name. [15]

1989		tendon
筋	Bamboo . . . part of the body . . . power. [12]	

LESSON 26

IT SHOULD come as no surprise that this lesson, which brings us to the primitive element for *person*, is rather long—73 new characters in all. Recall the advice given in FRAME 736 about selecting a particularly colorful acquaintance or member of your family for using in all the stories that involve the *person*.

1990 伍		V
	As with *II* in FRAME 1629, the key word represents the writing of the number "5" for official documents. The elements: *person . . . five*. [6]	
1991 仇		animosity
	Person . . . baseball (team). [4]	
1992 倡		start (v.)
	Person . . . prosperous. [10]	
1993 伯		father's older brother
	Person . . . dove. [7]	
1994 仲		mid-
	The key word is used in phrases like **mid**summer and **mid**-autumn. Its elements: *person . . . middle*. [6]	
1995 估		estimate (v.)
	Person . . . ancient. [7]	
1996 偵		detect
	Person . . . chaste. Hint: associate the key word with the work **detect**ives do. [11]	

1997 俱	altogether (ADV.)
Person . . . tool. [10]	

1998 側	lateral (ADJ.)
Person . . . rule. [11]	

1999 佑	bless
Person . . . right. [7]	

2000 佐	assistant
Person . . . left. [7]	

2001 仔	meticulous
Person . . . child. [5]	

2002 俏	comely
Person . . . candle. [9]	

2003 倘	if
Person . . . esteem. [10]	

2004 倚	count on
Person . . . strange. [10]	

2005 佳	superb
Person . . . bricks. [8]	

2006 侍	serve
Person . . . Buddhist temple. [8]	

2007 伙	mate (N.)
Person . . . fire. Let the key word **mate** suggest a partner or associate. [6]	

2008 宿	stay overnight *House . . . person . . . hundred.* [11]
2009 伏	bend over *Person . . . chihuahua.* [6]
2010 袱	wrapping cloth *Cloak . . . bend over.* [11]
2011 偷	steal [v.] *Person . . . slaughterhouse.* [11]
2012 伐	fell *Person . . . fiesta.* Hint: recall the German legend of the English missionary, Saint Boniface, who **felled** the sacred oak tree dedicated to Thor at Geismar (in lower Hessia), occasioning a great *fiesta* for the Christians in the neighborhood to mark the defeat of their pagan competition. Be sure to fit your special *person* into the story if you use it. [6]
2013 佩	wear at the waist *Person . . . wind . . . ceiling . . . towel.* Think of things like guns and swords that a swashbuckler might **wear at the waist**. [8]
2014 佈	announce *Person . . . cloth.* [7]
2015 僑	live abroad *Person . . . angel.* [14]
2016 億	one hundred million *Person . . . idea.* [15]

2017	incline (v.)
傾	Take this key word in its literal sense of *to lean to one side*. The elements: *person . . . 100 Chinese acres*. [13]

2018	insult (v.)
侮	*Person . . . every*. [9]

2019	times
倍	*Person . . . muzzle*. Think of this character as referring to the number of occurrences of an event. [10]

2020	mimic (v.)
仿	*Person . . . compass*. [6]

2021	haughty
傲	*Person . . . soil . . . release*. The combination of the two elements on the right previously appeared in *stew* (FRAME 1701). [13]

2022	Buddhist monk
僧	*Person . . . increase*. [14]

2023	without haste
悠	*Person . . . walking stick . . . taskmaster . . . heart*. Note that the three elements in the top half of this character appeared twice in Book 1 (FRAMES 744 and 1269). [11]

2024	Russia
俄	*Person . . . miser*. [9]

2025	rite
儀	*Person . . . righteousness*. Be careful not to confuse this key word with *ceremony* (FRAME 1069). [15]

2026	nephew
侄	*Person . . . until.* [8]
2027	immortal[N.]
仙	*Person . . . mountain.* [5]
2028	custom
俗	*Person . . . valley.* [9]
2029	repay
償	*Person . . . prize.* [17]
2030	for sleeping
臥	*Feudal official . . . person.* This character is used in many words having to do with sleep—things like bedrooms and Pullman cars. [8]
2031	close to
傍	*Person . . . Magellan.* [7]
❖ 奄	hang glider The hang glider is like a gigantic kite that is strong enough to support the weight of someone flying around on it. The image of the kite we used to learn the character for *electricity* (FRAME 399) will help here, but note that its final stroke has a bit more room here to extend out the top. Add to it the element for *large* (or, if you feel really inventive, a *St. Bernard dog*), and you will have your hang glider. [8] 大　奄
2032	we (exclusive)
俺	This character should be taken as forming a pair with *we (inclusive)* (FRAME 1503). There the person or persons spoken to were

included; here they are excluded. The elements: *person . . . hang glider.* [10]

2033	inundate
淹	*Water . . . hang glider.* [11]

2034	conceal
掩	*Fingers . . . hang glider.* [11]

❖ 崔	pterodactyl

Though scientists classify the **pterodactyl** as a kind of winged lizard, we know from this character that it is actually a distant cousin of the *turkey* that hovers around the *mountains* in search of its prey. [11]

山　崔

2035	prod (v.)
催	*Person . . . pterodactyl.* [13]

2036	wreck (v.)
摧	*Fingers . . . pterodactyl.* [14]

2037	take along
攜	*Wreck . . . hood . . . animal legs . . . mouth.* Note that the *human legs* in the printed form turn into *animal legs* in the hand-drawn form. [21]

扌　摧　攜　攜　攜

2038	symbol
符	*Bamboo . . . pay.* [11]

2039	loan (N.)
貸	*Substitute for . . . shells.* [12]

2040 荷	Holland
	This character on its own is used as an abbreviation for the Netherlands, although its pronunciation relies on the older name: **Holland**. *Flowers . . . whatwhichwhowherewhy?*. [11]

2041 仗	battle (N.)
	Person . . . 100 Chinese inches. [5]

2042 杖	cane
	Tree . . . 100 Chinese inches. This character has the same meaning as the primitive element we have called *walking stick*, so be sure to keep the two distinct. [7]

2043 夾	press from both sides
	Two persons in an elevator with a *St. Bernard dog* are **pressing from both sides** against the gentle creature to taunt it. To be continued.... [7] 一　尓　夾　夾

2044 俠	chivalrous person
	Now to continue from the previous frame, the two thimbleheads taunting the poor St. Bernard dog by *pressing from both sides* have not noticed that a *person* is behind them in the same elevator. It is none other than a **chivalrous person** in Arthurian armor sitting astride a great white stallion: Sir Liftsalot, who rides the elevators in search of villians engaged in animal harassment. Who said chivalry is dead! [9]

2045 頰	cheek
	Press from both sides . . . head. [16]

2046 狹	narrow (ADJ.)
	Packs of wild dogs . . . press from both sides. [10]

2047	coerce
挾	*Fingers . . . press from both sides.* [10]

2048	gorge (N.)
峽	*Mountains . . . press from both sides.* [10]

2049	umbrella
傘	*Umbrella . . . needle . . . four persons.* This is the full character from which the primitive element *umbrella* was derived. [12]

2050	assemble
聚	This character is simpler than it looks. The *take* on the top is familiar enough. The bottom half appeared earlier as the bottom half of *multitude* (FRAME 784). [14]

取　取　聚　聚　聚

2051	frustrate
挫	*Fingers . . . sit.* [10]

2052	saber
劍	*Debate . . . saber.* This is the character from which the primitive of the same name was derived in Book 1. [15]

2053	restrain
斂	Think of the *taskmaster* as teaching you to **restrain** yourself from going after your opponent with a chair during a *debate* in which you are clearly losing. [17]

2054	pick up (V.)
撿	The character means to **pick up** small objects with one's *fingers*. Here we see a rowdy audience so upset with the opponents in a political *debate* that they start to *pick up* tomatoes or whatever is close at hand to toss at the stage. [16]

2055 簽	sign [v.] Prior to participation in the annual *debate* of the Oriental Society, candidates must first qualify by shimmying up a twelve-foot stalk of *bamboo*, brush in mouth, to **sign** their names on a ledger at the top. [19]
2056 儉	thrifty *Person . . . debate.* [15]
2057 萊	lambsquarters The primitive elements that make up this character, *flowers* and *come*, are easier than the key word, which is not likely to be familiar to any but the botanically inclined. **Lambsquarters** is, in fact, a plant similar to the pigweed. The character is used mainly for its phonetic value in rendering foreign names. [12] ⺿　　萊
2058 葛	kudzu *Flowers . . . siesta.* [13]
2059 褐	brown *Cloak . . . siesta.* [14]
2060 竭	use up *Vase . . . siesta.* [14]
2061 歇	take a rest *Siesta . . . yawn.* [13]
2062 揭	reveal Gingerly lift up with your *fingers* the sombrero of that fellow over there leaning against the wall for a *siesta*, to **reveal** that it is actually an entire family taking a communal rest from the labors of the day. [12]

LESSON 27

2063 淫	promiscuous *Water . . . vulture . . . porter.* [11]
2064 挺	erect ^(ADJ.) *Fingers . . . royal court.* [10]
2065 瓦	tile The **tile** in this character combines four primitive elements: *ceiling . . . plow . . . fishhook . . .* and *drop of.* Since the drawing is a little unexpected, be sure to arrange your story to fit the stroke order. [4] 一　厂　瓦　瓦
2066 瓷	porcelain *Secondary . . . tile.* [10]
2067 瓶	bottle *Puzzle . . . tile.* [10]
2068 鋁	aluminium *Metal . . . spine.* [15]
2069 宮	palace Here a **palace** is composed of *house* and *spine.* [10]
2070 瑩	lustrous *Firehouse . . . jade.* [15]
2071 螢	firefly *Firehouse . . . insect.* [16]

2072		scoop up
撈	*Fingers . . . labor.* [15]	
2073		glowing
煥	*Fire . . . sled dogs.* [13]	

LESSON 28

2074

旋 — whirl (v.)

A banner . . . zoo. [11]

2075

吻 — kiss (v.)

Mouth . . . knot. [7]

2076

匆 — hurriedly

Think of tying a *knot* in your shoelaces so **hurriedly** that when your *eyedropper* falls out of your shirt pocket it gets tangled up in it. Makes it a little hard to put the drops in. [5]

　ノ　勹　勺　匆　匆

2077

錫 — tin

Metal . . . easy. [17]

2078

惕 — watchful

State of mind . . . easy. [11]

2079

屑 — bits

The sense of the key word is fragments, as in the phrase "**bits** and pieces." The elements: *flag . . . candle.* [10]

2080

尿 — urine

That rather special kind of *water* we call **urine** is used by many animals as a kind of *flag* to mark off their territory. [7]

2081

刷 — brush (N./V.)

Flag . . . towel . . . saber. This character and its key word need to be kept distinct from the primitive element for *brush* learned in Book 1. [8]

2082	rhinoceros
犀	Lacking a proper charging **rhinoceros** for the annual 4th of July parade, the townspeople put a *cow* on a bicycle with a patriotic *flag* attached to it and a little tape recorder playing "*Snowflakes keep falling on my head.*" [12]

尸　尸　尸　尸　尸　尸　犀

2083	tardy
遲	*Rhinoceros . . . road.* [15]

2084	leak (v.)
漏	*Water . . . flag . . . rain.* [14]

2085	fart (N.)
屁	*Flag . . . compare.* [7]

2086	footwear
履	*Flag . . . recover.* [15]

2087	excrement
屎	*Flag . . . rice.* [9]

2088	folding screen
屏	*Flag . . . puzzle.* [9]

2089	knuckle under
屈	*Flag . . . exit.* The key word is a colloquialism meaning to submit or yield. [8]

2090	excavate
掘	*Fingers . . . knuckle under.* [11]

2091	ruler
尺	Add a *flag* to your tape measure (the final stroke) to give yourself a more "patriotic" **ruler**, even if it is a little difficult to draw straight lines with. [4]

2092	eyebrows
眉	Over the *eyes* we see a *flag* divided into two colors. This is because the **eyebrows** are painted different colors, one of them red and the other blue. [9]
	㇆　㇒刁　㇕刁　尸　眉

2093	flatter
媚	*Woman . . . eyebrows.* [12]

2094	shoulder (N.)
肩	*Door . . . flesh.* [8]

2095	jealous of
妒	*Woman . . . door.* [7]

2096	tears
淚	*Water . . . door . . . chihuahua.* [11]

2097	enlighten
啓	*Door . . . taskmaster . . . mouth.* [11]

2098	fan (N.)
扇	*Door . . . wings.* [10]

LESSON 29

2099 奈	**can't help but** *St. Bernard dog . . . altar.* [8]
2100 款	**funds** *Soldier . . . altar . . . yawn.* The key word here refers to sums of money. [12]
2101 祟	**evil spirit** *Exit . . . altar.* [10]
2102 祝	**wish well** *Altar . . . teenager.* The meaning of the key word is to **wish** someone **well**. [9]
2103 祥	**propitious** *Altar . . . sheep.* [10]
2104 祕	**confidential** *Altar . . . certainly.* [9]
❖ 尉	**Cardinal Richelieu** From your reading of "The Three Musketeers," you may remember **Cardinal Richelieu** as the ambitious and high-ranking churchman who wielded political power second only to the king himself. The character symbolizes this by showing a *flag* that has been spread over and *glued* to an *altar.* [11] 尸　尽　尉
2105 慰	**console** (v.) *Cardinal Richelieu . . . heart.* [15]

2106 蔚	*Flowers . . . Cardinal Richelieu.* [15]	luxuriant
2107 蒜	*Flowers . . . two altars.* [14]	garlic
2108 棕	*Tree . . . religion.* [12]	palm tree
2109 宙	*House . . . sprout.* [8]	universe
2110 軸	*Car . . . sprout.* [12]	axle
2111 袖	*Cloak . . . sprout.* [10]	sleeve
2112 笛	*Bamboo . . . sprout.* [11]	flute
2113 坤	*Soil . . . monkey.* [8]	female
2114 呻	*Mouth . . . monkey.* [8]	groan
2115 暢	To get the sense of this key word, think of something without bumps or obstructions, perhaps something like the tail of a *monkey* or a *piglet.* [14]	smooth

2116 夥	**partnership**

When we think of a **partnership** or company, we think of the business tycoons who come together to sell things in great quantity—like bananas and oranges. Here we see the *fruits* fighting back, with *many* of them joining forces to form a **partnership** of their own and protect themselves against extradition without the right to "habeas fructum." [11]

2117 巢	**nest** (N.)

Stream . . . fruit. [11]

2118 棵	**flora**

Tree . . . fruit. This is another one of those "measure words" we have run into occasionally. This one is used for green, non-fauna living things like trees and grasses. [12]

2119 裸	**naked**

Cloak . . . fruit. [13]

2120 裹	**envelop**

The basic idea of this key word is to encase something completely with a covering. Its elements: *top hat and scarf . . . fruit.* Observe how the primitive for *fruit* detaches the final two strokes of the "tree," as in the primitive element for a *wooden pole*, and shortens the vertical center stroke. [14]

亠 東 裹

LESSON 30

2121 析	analyze *Tree . . . tomahawk.* [8]
2122 晰	distinct *Sun . . . analyze.* If it is any help, the father of modern philosophy, René Descartes, based his thought on the search for "clear and **distinct** ideas." [12]
2123 芹	celery *Flowers . . . tomahawk.* [8]
2124 折	discount ^(N.) *Fingers . . . tomahawk.* [7]
2125 哲	philosopher *Discount . . . mouth.* [10]
2126 逝	pass away *Discount . . . road.* [10]
2127 誓	vow ^(N./V.) *Discount . . . words.* [14]
2128 欣	elated *Tomahawk . . . yawn.* [8]
2129 掀	uncover *Fingers . . . elated.* [11]

| 2130 祈 | supplicate |
| Altar . . . tomahawk. [8] | |

| 2131 慚 | conscience-stricken |
| State of mind . . . hew. [14] | |

| 2132 嶄 | towering |
| Mountain . . . hew. [14] | |

| 2133 拆 | take apart |
| Fingers . . . reprimand. [8] | |

| 2134 炸 | blow up |
| Fire . . . saw. The key word refers not to what you do to a balloon, but what will happen to a balloon if you do it too much. [9] | |

| 2135 詐 | swindle |
| Words . . . saw. [12] | |

| 2136 妻 | wife |
| Needle . . . broom . . . woman. Although the elements fit together, note the breakdown in stroke order. [8] | |

一　彐　圭　妻

| 2137 凄 | miserable |
| Water . . . wife. [11] | |

| 2138 棲 | perch (v.) |
| Birds are not the only things to **perch** in *trees*, as we see in this character. A disgruntled *wife* pondering her next move has taken her place alongside a row of robins on a branch of the oak *tree* in the garden. [12] | |

2139 goblin

煞 Bound up . . . broom . . . taskmaster . . . cooking fire. [13]

2140 nimble

捷 To remember this character, think of the famous calligrapher and founder of the esoteric Buddhist tradition, Kūkai. He is said to have been able to write five poems simultaneously by holding brushes in his mouth, hands, and feet. You do him one better by having your *fingers* fitted out with *ten* small *brooms*. Dip them in ink and watch as they move across the paper all at once with lightning speed, each leaving behind a distinct shape. At first it looks like no more than a smudgy *trail of footprints*, but if you look closely, you will see that they are Chinese characters arranged into a classical poem. Now that is much more **nimble** than Jack and his candlestick! [11]

扌 扩 扗 挂 捗 捷 捷

2141 wield

秉 A *broom* is drawn inside of the primitive for *wild rice*. Note the doubling up. [8]

丿 二 彐 手 秉 秉

2142 peel off

剝 Snowman . . . saber. [10]

2143 collection

彙 The key word refers to things collected, not the process of collecting. What kind of **collection** could one be aiming at here, sweeping up *crowns* and *fruit* with a *whisk broom*? [13]

2144 double (ADJ.)

兼 At the top we have the *animal horns* and the single horizontal stroke to give them something to hang onto. Below that, we see one *rake* with two handles. Finally, we see a pair of strokes splitting away from each of the handles, indicating that they are both splitting under the pressure. The composite picture is of someone leading a **double** life and splitting apart at the seams. Take the time to find this sense in the character and it will be easy to remember, despite initial appearances. [10]

丷 ⺍ 当 단 넘 並 兼

2145 賺	earn
	Shells . . . double. [17]
2146 嫌	dislike (v.)
	Woman . . . double. [13]
2147 謙	unassuming
	Words . . . double. [17]
2148 歉	apology
	Double . . . yawn. [14]
2149 廉	inexpensive
	Cave . . . double. [13]
2150 鎌	sickle
	Metal . . . inexpensive. [18]
2151 簾	drapes
	Bamboo . . . inexpensive. [19]
2152 睜	unshut (v.)
	Eyeballs . . . contend. As you might have guessed from the opening primitive element, this character refers to what your eyes do when you open them. [13]

2153	struggle [v.]
掙	Fingers . . . contend. [11]

2154	Chinese zither
箏	Bamboo . . . contend. [14]

2155	pool [N.]
塘	News flash! In a stunning reversal of the history of sport, archaeologists working on a site in central China recently un*earth*ed artifacts confirming that the origins of synchronized swimming go back to the *Tang* Dynasty. The presence of skimpy swimsuits and nose plugs lying at the bottom of what was once a natural *pool* is said to constitute persuasive scientific evidence that they perished in sync. [13]

❖	butler
隶	The **butler** pulls a miniature *rake* out of his waistcoat to scrape the *snowflakes* from the coats of visitors to the mansion.

We already met this combination in Book 1 (FRAME 881). Note how the last stroke of *rake* serves as the first stroke of *snowflakes*. [8]

彐　肀　聿　隶

2156	arrest [v.]
逮	Butler . . . road. [11]

2157	bondservant
隸	Tree . . . altar . . . butler. [17]

2158	generous
慷	State of mind . . . hale. [14]

2159	chaff
糠	Rice . . . hale. [17]

| 2160 耍 | **mess around** The hint of mischief in the key word is best managed by imagining yourself teasing a *woman* you know by going after her *combs*. You **mess around** with them by soaking them in dye, hair remover, and catnip. [9] |

| 2161 耐 | **-proof** The key word is a suffix used to indicate "resistant to" or "protected against," as in the words rust**proof**, water**proof**, and fire**proof**. It is composed of: *comb . . . glue.* [9] |

| 2162 喘 | **wheeze** *Mouth . . . prospector.* [12] |

| 2163 揣 | **conjecture** (v.) *Fingers . . . prospector.* [12] |

| ❖ 曹 | **cadet** The three primitive elements for **cadet** suggest a young recruit going through his "hazing." *One bent day.* What a perfect way to describe this brief but infantile chapter in military training. If you look at the printed form, you can see the young **cadet** standing proud and erect after having passed the initiation ritual, broad at the shoulders and narrow at the waist. [11]
 一　厂　㫕　甫　曲　曲　曹 |

| 2164 糟 | **messed up** The slang expression of this character's key word refers to a person or situation that has landed in a rather wretched state. Its elements are: *rice . . . cadet.* [17] |

| 2165 遭 | **meet with** The sense of this key word is a chance encounter, usually negative, as when one **meets with** misfortune or disaster. Its elements: *cadet . . . road.* [14] |

2166 槽	trough
Tree . . . cadet. [15]	

2167 抖	quiver (v.)
Fingers . . . Big Dipper. [7]	

2168 庸	mediocre
Cave . . . rake . . . rack. The only thing you have to watch out for here is the handle of the *rake*, which is drawn last. [11]	

户 肀 肀 庸

2169 傭	put to work
Person . . . mediocre. [13]	

2170 甩	fling (v.)
Think of this character as a *rack* of "tails" of various beasts. [5]	

2171	rue (v.)
惜	*State of mind . . . times past.* The sense of the key word is to regret the loss of something cherished. [11]

2172	arrange
措	*Fingers . . . times past.* [11]

2173	forsake
棄	*Infant . . . twenty . . . tree.* [12]

亠　亠　产　弃　吞　查　章
章　棄

2174	swallow (N.)
燕	This key word refers to the bird, and the elements suggest that a score of them are being boiled in order to be "swallowed" by their human predators. The primitives: *Twenty . . . mouth . . . north . . . cooking fire.* Note how the *mouth* is placed between the two sides of *north*, for which you may find it helpful to revert to the image of *two people sitting on the ground* back to back, as explained in FRAME 420. [16]

廿　甘　苫　燕　燕

2175	screen (v.)
遮	*Caverns . . . cooking fire . . . road.* [14]

2176	littoral (N.)
畔	*Rice field . . . half.* The key word here is used principally for areas that border a body of water. [10]

2177	blend (v.)
拌	Fingers . . . half. [8]

2178	betray
叛	Half . . . against. [9]

2179	voucher
券	Quarter . . . dagger. [8]

2180	rattan
藤	Flower . . . moon . . . quarter . . . snowflakes. [19]

2181	state of affairs
狀	Bunk beds . . . chihuahua. [8]

2182	wall
牆	Bunk beds . . . soil . . . assembly line . . . return. [17]

爿　爿⁺　爿⁺　牂　牂　牆

2183	old cooking pot
鼎	Eyeball . . . bunk beds . . . slice. The *eyeball* takes up so much space that the second stroke of *bunk beds* and the first stroke of *slice* need to be shortened. Take particular care with the stroke order here. [13]

目　目　目　鼎　鼎　鼎ʼ　鼎ʼ

鼎　鼎

❖	dunce
彗	It should not be hard to work the primitive elements—*broom* . . . *crown* . . . *crotch*—into a colorful image of the class **dunce** (especially if you ever had to play the role yourself). [7]

ヨ　ヨ　灵

2184 寝	get some shuteye
	House . . . bunk beds . . . dunce. [14]

2185 侵	invade
	Person . . . dunce. [9]

2186 浸	immerse
	Water . . . dunce. [10]

❖ 臧

surfboarding

This character is not as unfamiliar as it looks at first. After the first two strokes of *parade*, you draw in the primitive for *bunk beds*, letting the second stroke double up with the second stroke of *parade*. Then comes the *feudal official*, and finally the rest of *parade*.

This *parade* of *feudal officials* are all running at top speed, *bunk beds* in hand, toward the beach, en route to the annual **surfboarding** competition. The sport was short-lived because of the high morality rate among the athletes. Only several centuries later did the Hawaiians rescue the art of **surfboarding** by replacing the box springs, mattress, and bedstead with a flat plank. [14]

厂　广　疒　疒　疟　臧

2187 贜	stolen goods
	Shells . . . surfboarding. [21]

2188 藏	hide (v.)
	Flowers . . . surfboarding. [18]

2189 臟	guts
	Flesh . . . hide. [21]

2190	award (N.)
獎	General . . . St. Bernard dog. [15]

2191	thick liquid
漿	General . . . water. [15]

2192	oar
槳	General . . . tree. [15]

2193	Jiang
蔣	Jiang is the surname of **General**issimo Chiang Kai-shek (or as today's orthography has him, **Jiang** Jieshi), head of the Nationalist Government of the Republic of China until 1975. Conveniently, the primitive elements are: *flowers . . . General.* [15]

2194	abyss
淵	The only thing you have to watch out for with this character is the drawing order of the complex of elements to the right. To begin with, ignore the elements for *slice* and *bunk beds* learned earlier. Now think of the single horizontal stroke that is drawn in order as you work your way down top to bottom as a tightrope that is stretched across a great **abyss**. The *water* to the left represents the dribble of a stream flowing at the bottom of the **abyss**, all that is left of the mighty *waters* that originally carved it out. [12]

汁 氵 氵丨 氵丨 氵丨 沪 沪 淵 淵 淵

2195	solemn
肅	Unlike you, who barefooted it across the *abyss* unaided, the tightrope walker in this frame is the lead in a **solemn** proces-

sion of a whole retinue of tightrope walkers making their way across the Grand Canyon. She uses the *rake* as a balancing pole. Add a little background music and the scene takes on a **solemn** dignity befitting that most glorious of holes in the ground. We give the full drawing order to avoid any confusion and clarify the difference from the character in the previous frame. [13]

❖ In connection with the explanation above, the meaning of this character will change to *Grand Canyon* when it is used as a primitive element.

2196	howl [v.]
嘯	*Mouth . . . Grand Canyon.* There are lots of ways to **howl** and lots of things that are said to **howl**. No single English word can handle everything from the rushing of the wind to the screaming of a wild animal and the roaring of the sea. But this character does just that. [16]
2197	desolate
蕭	*Flowers . . . Grand Canyon.* [17]
2198	rust [N./V.]
鏽	*Metal . . . Grand Canyon.* [21]
2199	sesame
芝	*Flowers . . . sign of Zorro.* [7]
2200	devalue
貶	*Shells . . . weary.* [11]
2201	nonspecific
泛	*Water . . . weary.* [7]

2202   askew

歪   *No . . . correct.* [9]

LESSON 32

2203 矯	rectify *Dart . . . angel.* [17]
2204 矮	short of stature *Dart . . . committee.* [13]
❖ 矣	crossbow If you've ever drawn back a **crossbow**, the elements *elbow* and *dart* should be easy enough to associate with this primitive element. [7] <div align="center">厶 矣</div>
2205 唉	sigh—ay-ay *Mouth . . . crossbow.* The key word is meant to simulate the sad, sighing sound issuing forth from the *mouth* of a warrior whose *crossbow* has broken down after the expiration of the warranty. **Ay-ay-ay-ay-aaaaaaaaaaay.** [10]
2206 埃	fine dust *Soil . . . crossbow.* [10]
2207 挨	suffer *Fingers . . . crossbow.* [10]
2208 簇	cluster (N.) *Bamboo . . . tribe.* [17]
2209 茅	thatch (N.) *Flowers . . . spear.* [9]

2210 橘	tangerine
	Tree . . . spear . . . motorcycle helmet . . . animal legs . . . mouth. You may want to return to FRAME 416 of Book 1 to recall how you combined the final elements into a memorable image. There you will see, too, how the *human legs* in the printed form change to *animal legs* in the hand-drawn form. [16]

2211 舒	relax
	Abode . . . bestow. [12]

2212 弘	noble
	Bow . . . elbow. [5]

2213 夷	barbarian
	St. Bernard dog . . . bow. Note how the stroke order follows the principles of writing and does not draw the primitive elements separately. [6]

一　弓　夷　夷

2214 姨	maternal aunt
	Woman . . . barbarian. [9]

❖ 畺	family feud
	Two *rice fields*, each of them separated by a stone wall on the north and another on the south (the three *ones*) create an image of the most famous **family feud** in American history, that between the Hatfields and McCoys. [13]

一　畾　畕　畕　畺

2215 疆	dividing line
	Bow . . . soil . . . family feud. Think of this key word as referring to a boundary or border. [19]

2216 僵	stiff (ADJ.) *Person . . . family feud.* [15]
2217 薑	ginger *Flowers . . . family feud.* [17]
2218 粥	porridge *Two bows . . . rice.* [12] 弓　粥　粥
2219 沸	bring to a boil *Water . . . dollar sign.* [8]
2220 拂	caress (v.) *Fingers . . . dollar sign.* [8]
2221 剃	shave (v.) *Younger brother . . . saber.* [9]
2222 涕	snot The reason *younger brother* can be such a pain in the neck, a thorn, or bothersome pest—in short, such a "snot"—must have something to do with the disgusting drops of *water* that leak from people's nostrils, which is in fact the **snot** this character refers to. [10]
2223 梯	ladder *Tree . . . younger brother.* [11]
2224 朽	decayed *Tree . . . snare.* As the primitive on the left suggests, this character often applies to wood. The broader sense of the key word,

which includes the way people get **decayed** by senility or old age, may be helpful in making your story. [6]

| 2225 | employ^(v.) |

聸

Though you may "hire" a laborer, you use the high-sounding **employ** to take on people of higher status in the organization. Its elements: *ear . . . sprout . . . snare.* [13]

| 2226 | sacrifice^(v.) |

犠

Like the character in FRAME 842, this one can be used in connection with *animal sacrifices,* but it can also mean to **sacrifice** something for the sake of something else of higher value. Its elements: *cow . . . sheep . . . wild rice . . . snare . . . fiesta.* Take care in drawing the second stroke of the primitive for *wild rice.* It is stretched out to double up as the first stroke of *fiesta.* [20]

| 2227 | elder sister |

姉

To complement the older brother (FRAME 89) and elder brother (101), we need an older sister (1298) and now an **elder sister**. The combination of elements to the right of *woman* is a rare combination, and for that reason special attention should be given to its drawing. The first two strokes on the right are somewhat like a *snare* except that the first stroke is drawn right to left, like *drag.* So think of it as a *snare* you are *dragging* by hand along the ground. The character finishes with what are actually the last two strokes of a *genie,* who has been caught in the *snare* and is wiggling to get free. What all this has to do with your **elder sister** we leave to you to decide. [7]

女 女 姉 姉 姉

LESSON 33

2228 躺	lie down *Somebody . . . esteem.* [15]
2229 躲	dodge (v.) *Somebody . . . flouds.* [13]
2230 躬	stoop (v.) *Somebody . . . bow.* [10]
2231 嗜	hanker *Mouth . . . old man . . . tongue wagging in the mouth.* [13]
2232 拷	flog *Fingers . . . take an exam.* [9]
2233 暑	summer heat *Sun . . . puppet.* [12]
2234 睹	behold *Eyeballs . . . puppet.* [13]
2235 賭	gamble (v.) *Shells . . . puppet.* [15]
2236 奢	extravagant *St. Bernard dog . . . puppet.* [11]
2237 堵	stop up *Soil . . . puppet.* [11]

2238 煮	boil [v.]
	Puppet . . . cooking fire. [12]

2239 諸	various
	Words . . . puppet. [15]

2240 儲	put in storage
	Person . . . various. [17]

2241 屠	slaughter
	Flag . . . puppet. [11]

2242 署	add your John Hancock
	Net . . . puppet. [13]

2243 薯	yam
	Flowers . . . add your John Hancock. [17]

2244 歸	come back
	Maestro . . . footprint . . . broom . . . apron. [18]

2245 篩	sift
	Bamboo . . . teacher. [16]

2246 棺	coffin
	Tree . . . bureaucrat. [12]

2247 爹	dad
	Father . . . many. [10]

2248 斧	axe
	Father . . . tomahawk. [8]

2249 咬	bite (v.) *Mouth . . . mingle.* [9]
2250 狡	sly *Pack of wild dogs . . . mingle.* [9]
2251 趴	prostrate oneself *Wooden leg . . . eight.* [9]
2252 踏	trample *Wooden leg . . . water . . . sun.* [15]
2253 踐	tread on *Wooden leg . . . float.* [15]
2254 蹄	hoof *Wooden leg . . . sovereign.* [16]
2255 捉	catch (v.) In learning this character, think of how you **catch** animals or insects. The elements: *fingers . . . lower leg.* [10]
2256 踩	step on *Wooden leg . . . pluck.* [15]
2257 蹦	hop (v.) *Wooden leg . . . crumble.* [18]
2258 跌	slump (v.) *Wooden leg . . . lose.* Take this key word in the sense in which prices or productivity can fall or **slump**. [12]

2259	urge (v.)
促	*Person . . . lower leg.* [9]

2260	kick (v.)
踢	*Wooden leg . . . easy.* [15]

❖	wood pulp
槀	Let this primitive mean **wood pulp**, from the fact that it is one of the many *goods* produced from *trees.* [13]

品　槀

2261	impetuous
躁	*Wooden leg . . . wood pulp.* [20]

2262	chirping (N.)
噪	*Mouth . . . wood pulp.* You might just ignore the compound primitive altogether and look instead at all the *mouths* around and in the *tree.* [16]

2263	bath
澡	*Water . . . wood pulp.* [16]

2264	algae
藻	*Flowers . . . bath.* [20]

2265	exercise (N.)
操	*Fingers . . . wood pulp.* [16]

2266	parched
燥	*Fire . . . wood pulp.* [17]

❖ 翟	**headdress** The *feathers* of the *turkey* (with the rest of the bird attached) are used to make a one-of-a-kind **headdress**. [14] 羽　翟
2267 躍	**leap** (v.) *Wooden leg . . . headdress.* [21]
2268 戳	**jab** (v.) *Headdress . . . fiesta.* [18]
2269 耀	**show off** (v.) *Ray . . . headdress.* [20]
2270 猾	**cunning** *Pack of wild dogs . . . skeleton.* [13]
2271 髓	**marrow** *Skeleton . . . left . . . flesh . . . road.* [22]
2272 髒	**dirty** *Skeleton . . . inter.* [23]
2273 渦	**whirlpool** *Water . . . jawbone.* [12]
2274 鍋	**pot** *Metal . . . jawbone.* Be sure to create an image of a cooking **pot** distinct from the *old cooking pot* (FRAME 2147). [17]
2275 蝸	**snail** *Insect . . . jawbone.* [15]

2276		misfortune
禍	*Altar . . . jawbone.* [13]	

LESSON 34

2277 陌	footpath *Pinnacle . . . hundred.* [9]
2278 隙	rift (N.) The key word refers to a gap or a break. Its elements: *pinnacle . . . few . . . spring.* Note that the final stroke of *few* makes the first stroke of *spring* unnecessary. [14]
2279 陡	steep *Pinnacle . . . walk.* [10]
2280 障	barrier *Pinnacle . . . chapter.* [14]
2281 陪	accompany *Pinnacle . . . muzzle.* [11]
2282 隧	tunnel (N.) *Pinnacle . . . satisfy.* [15]
2283 墜	plunge (V.) The sense of the key word is to fall precipitously. The elements: *team . . . ground.* [15]
2284 陋	undesirable *Pinnacle . . . third . . . fishhook.* The drawing order following the primitives. [9]
2285 挖	dig (V.) *Fingers . . . hole . . . fishhook.* [9]

2286 窯	kiln

Hole . . . sheep . . . cooking fire. [15]

2287 窺	peep (v.)

The character refers to spying through a **peep**hole, but here we can see a lawyer **peep** through the *regulations* in search of a *hole* for his corrupt client to crawl through. [16]

2288 窟	den

The key word is used for hideaways of bandits, gangsters, and the like. Its primitives: *hole . . . knuckle under.* [13]

2289 窄	strait (ADJ.)

This rather antique-sounding word refers to something "not wide." Be sure to keep your image distinct from the one you made for the character that means *narrow* (FRAME 2049). Its elements: *hole . . . saw.* [10]

2290 榨	extract (v.)

Tree . . . strait. Think of the physical act of pressing or squeezing to **extract** one thing from another, like juice from oranges. [14]

2291 窘	poverty-stricken

Hole . . . monarch. [12]

2292 窮	poor

Hole . . . stoop. The key word means having little money, goods, or other means of support. [15]

2293 窩	hollow (N.)

Just as the character for *mouth* could refer to a whole range of things, this one can appear in compounds for things that have a **hollow**—everything from a hornets' nest to a dimple to a fox's lair. Take your pick! *Hole . . . jawbone.* [14]

2294

腔   *Flesh . . . empty.* [12]

body cavity

LESSON 35

2295 累	**tired** *Rice field . . . thread.* Note that the primitive elements are exactly the same as those for *fine* (FRAME 1018), only arranged differently. [11]
2296 螺	**spiral shell** *Insect . . . tired.* [17]
2297 紗	**yarn** *Thread . . . few.* The primitive on the left is enough to warn us that this character does not refer to tall tales. Be sure to keep your image distinct from that for the primitive of the same meaning. [10]
2298 綽	**ample** *Thread . . . eminent.* [14]
2299 紹	**acquaint** *Thread . . . summon.* [11]
2300 絮	**long-winded** *Be like . . . thread.* [12]
2301 繞	**go around** *Thread . . . Pigpen.* The key word means to detour or circumvent. [18]
2302 紮	**bind** (v.) *Tree . . . fishhook . . . thread.* [11]

2303 **continuous**

綿 If you think of a single, unbroken, **continuous** piece of *thread* being used to make all the *white towels* in your house. It might be efficient, but it could cause problems when it comes to doing the laundry. [14]

2304 **paint** (V.)

繪 You can **paint** to coat a wall or you can **paint** to create art. This character refers to the latter. *Thread . . . meeting.* [19]

2305 **web**

絡 *Thread . . . each.* [12]

2306 **silk fabric**

綢 *Thread . . . lap.* [14]

2307 **down** (N.)

絨 *Thread . . . fiesta . . . needle.* [12]

2308 **conclude**

締 Let this key word connote what people do when they formalize a treaty, an alliance, an association, and so forth. Its elements are: *thread . . . sovereign.* [15]

2309 **purple**

紫 *This (literary) . . . thread.* Although you will not meet any examples in these volumes, it may help to think of the "**purple** prose" of those inferior writers who pile clumsy cliches on top of one another from the crack of a rosy-fingered dawn till the fall of the final curtain on a dark and stormy night, or otherwise shamelessly ornament and exaggerate with a complete lack of literary conscience. [12]

2310 繁 **numerous**

Quick-witted . . . thread. [17]

2311 紡 **spin** (v.)

For the character that means to **spin** *thread* and other fibers, we have the elements: *thread . . . compass.* [10]

2312 繭 **cocoon**

Though it's a good thing that the primitive for **cocoon** has been radically abbreviated from this, its full form as a character, the story it holds is a charming one. The silkworm (*insect*) eats the leaves of the mulberry bush (the *flowers*), digests them and transforms them into *thread* with which it spins about itself, in mystic wisdom, its own coffin (the *hood*). The *walking stick* that separates the two elements helps the picture of the little worm cutting itself off from contact with the outside world, but as a character stroke, it is a clear exception. [19]

2313 纏 **wind around**

Thread . . . cave . . . computer . . . human legs . . . soil. [21]

2314 緻 **delicate**

Thread . . . bring about. [16]

2315 繫 **fasten**

Car . . . mountain . . . missile . . . thread. Note the doubling up of the final stroke of *car* and the first of *mountain.* [19]

2316 納 **let in**

Thread . . . internal. The sense of the key word is to admit or receive someone or something. [10]

2317 紛	disorderly *Thread . . . part.* [10]
2318 縮	shrink (v.) *Thread . . . stay overnight* [17]
2319 綜	sum up *Thread . . . religion.* [14]
2320 紳	gentry *Thread . . . monkey.* In Chinese nomenclature, the **gentry** was a class of individuals who had passed the bureaucratic examinations. [11]
2321 緣	reason (N.) Think of this key word as referring to the cause of things. The elements you have to work with are: *thread . . . whisk broom . . . sow.* The final stroke of the *whisk broom* doubles up with the first stroke of the *sow.* [15]
2322 緒	inception *Thread . . . puppet.* [14]
2323 絞	wring *Thread . . . mingle.* [12]
❖ 爰	migrating ducks This primitive is simplicity itself. It depicts bird *claws* (or in this case, duck *claws*) that are joined to one another. Note the extra horizontal stroke in the character for *friend*, which gives the appearance of a "two" in the middle of the character, further emphasizing the togetherness of the **migrating ducks.** [9] 爫　　爫　爫　爭　爰

2324 緩	unhurried
	Thread . . . migrating ducks. [15]

2325 暖	warm [ADJ.]
	Sun . . . migrating ducks. [13]

2326 援	provide assistance
	Fingers . . . migrating ducks. [12]

❖ 亠	chapel
	The *house* with the "cross" on the roof will serve us as a primitive element meaning **chapel**. While we have shied away from using pictographs, we think you will agree that seeing the "cross" as a replacement of the "chimney" atop the *house* is a helpful exception. [4]

+   亠 |

2327 索	large rope
	Chapel . . . thread. [10]

❖ 孛	Sunday school
	The *chapel* with the *children* inside becomes a primitive element meaning **Sunday school**. [7]

亠   孛 |

2328 勃	vibrant
	Sunday school . . . muscle. When you imagine this key word, think of something lively and pulsing with energy—whatever that may have to do with *Sunday school*. [9]

2329 脖	head-hinge
	The meaning of this character is actually the "neck," but we adjusted the key word to avoid confusing it with another char-

acter we will learn for *neck* later in this lesson (FRAME 2338).
We have adopted a technical term from the little-known clas-
sic "Very Gray Anatomy": a **head-hinge**. You may, if you wish,
replace it with a term of your own. **Head-stand** and **shoulder-
stump** come to mind as possibilities. In any case, its elements
are: *flesh . . . Sunday school.* [11]

❖
敫
homing pigeon

You might think here of the first **homing pigeon** in recorded
history: the *dove* that Noah *released* from the Ark in search of
dry land. The first time, it returned. After seven days, Noah
released the *dove* again, and this time it came back with an olive
branch in its beak. On the third and final flight, it did not return
and Noah knew that it had found land.

The combination of parts in this primitive element, you may
remember, was used with a quite different image in Book 1
(FRAME 464). [13]

白　臽　敫

2330

繳
shell out

The key word is used to **shell out** things like your hard-earned
cash. Its elements: *thread . . . homing pigeon.* [19]

2331

邀
request the presence of

Homing pigeon . . . road. [16]

2332

繡
embroidery

Thread . . . Grand Canyon. [19]

2333

蘿
edible root

This character figures in words for things like turnips and rad-
ishes. Its elements: *flowers . . . silk gauze.* [23]

2334

鑼
gong

Metal . . . silk gauze. [27]

2335 邏	make the rounds

The police ordered to **make the rounds** take their orders rather too literally, wrapping the *roads* round and round with *silk gauze*. [22]

2336 籮	bamboo basket

Bamboo . . . silk gauze. [25]

2337 蠻	barbaric

Needlepoint . . . insect. [25]

2338 頸	neck (N.)

Spool . . . head. [16]

2339 莖	plant stem

Flowers . . . spool. [11]

2340 勁	powerful

Spool . . . muscle. [9]

2341 徑	trail (N.)

Queue . . . spool. The key word in this frame should suggest a footpath, not an established overland route. [10]

2342 溪	creek

Water . . . vulture . . . cocoon . . . St. Bernard dog. We have met the combination of primitives on the right before in the character for *chicken* (FRAME 1037). [13]

2343 幼	young

Cocoon . . . muscle. [5]

2344 幽	secluded

Mountain . . . two cocoons. [9]

幺 丝 幽 幽

2345

濕   wet

Water . . . sun . . . two cocoons . . . cooking fire. [17]

2346

玄   mysterious

A *top hat* and a *cocoon* combine to create a **mysterious**-looking creature, something out of a science fiction horror movie. [5]

亠 玄

2347

畜   livestock

Mysterious . . . rice field. [10]

2348

蓄   save up

Flowers . . . livestock [14]

2349

牽   lead along

Mysterious . . . crown . . . cow. [11]

玄   牵   牽

2350

弦   bowstring

What is so *mysterious* about this **bowstring** is that it has been taken from the *bow* and used to string a cello, where it can make music and at the same time still be used by a virtuoso for sending arrows toward their target. Or, from the victim's viewpoint, "killing me softly, with his song." [8]

❖

茲   Mona Lisa

Note the doubling up of the element for *mysterious* here. Now if there is any work of art that qualifies as doubly *mysterious* (see FRAME 2346), it is Da Vinci's **Mona Lisa**. [9]

艹 茲 茲

2351 磁	magnetism
	Stone . . . Mona Lisa. Let the key word here refer to the physical quality of certain metals, not to charismatic personalities. [14]

2352 滋	nourish
	Water . . . Mona Lisa. [12]

2353 慈	kindhearted
	Mona Lisa . . . heart. [13]

2354 譏	deride
	Words . . . abacus. [19]

2355 爍	luminous
	Fire . . . music. [19]

2356 遜	modest
	Grandchild . . . road. [13]

LESSON 36

2357 卸	**unload** The left primitive is a union of a *stick horse* and a *footprint*. To the right, the *stamp*. [9]
2358 御	**imperial** *Queue . . . unload.* [12]
2359 禦	**withstand** *Imperial . . . altar.* [17]

2360 卵	**nest eggs** This character shows a *letter opener* with a couple of *drops* of something or other. The key word should give it away: it has been splattered with **nest eggs** you picked up from a nearby tree. As to what unfortunate creature had its offspring end up on a *letter opener* and what the owner of that desktop weapon had to do with it, these are matters better left to your imagination than to ours. [7]

´   ㇆   ㇏   纟   幻   卯   卵 |

❖ 孚	**fledglings** A *vulture* and a *child* combine to create a rather gruesome image of an aerie full of **fledglings**. [7]

爫   孚 |

2361 孵	**hatch** (v.) *Nest eggs . . . fledglings.* [14]

2362	breast
乳	*Fledglings . . . fishhook.* Don't confuse this full character with the primitive element for *breasts*. [8]

2363	float (v.)
浮	*Water . . . fledglings.* Be careful not to confuse this key word with the primitive noun we learned in Book 1 as *float*. [10]

2364	captive
俘	*Person . . . fledglings.* [9]

2365	minister
卿	*Letter opener. . . silver.* Be sure to locate the primitive for *silver* INSIDE the *letter opener*. The key word refers to a high-ranking government official in Chinese history. [10]

2366	trade (N.)
貿	*Letter opener . . . shells.* [12]

2367	pomegranate
榴	*Tree . . . stay.* [14]

2368	doubt (v.)
疑	The existential state in which one **doubts** everyone and everything is depicted here as *someone sitting on the ground* in the middle of a *zoo* with a *dart* in the bottom and a *chop* in the hand. Now how in the world did I ever get here? Is this real or am I dreaming? [14]

ヒ　矣　矣ᒿ　疑

❖ Used as a primitive element, this character will mean a *furled brow*, the kind that shows up when someone is beset by serious doubts.

2369 礙	obstruct *Stone . . . furled brow.* [19]
2370 凝	congeal *Ice . . . furled brow.* [16]
2371 擬	simulate *Fingers . . . furled brow.* [17]
2372 玲	exquisite *Jewel . . . orders.* [9]
2373 鈴	small bell *Metal . . . orders.* [13]
2374 伶	actor *Person . . . orders.* [7]
2375 嶺	mountain range *Mountain . . . collar.* [17]
2376 桶	bucket *Tree . . . chop-rack.* [11]
2377 誦	read aloud *Words . . . chop-rack.* [14]
2378 湧	gush (v.) *Water . . . courageous.* [12]
2379 踴	eagerly *Wooden leg . . . courageous.* [16]

2380 **exam paper**

卷 *Quarter . . . fingerprint.* [8]

2381 **circle** (N.)

圈 The key word refers both to the geometrical object and to a circumscribed group, as in one's "**circle** of friends." Its primitives: *pent in . . . exam paper.* [11]

2382 **roll up**

捲 *Fingers . . . exam paper.* [11]

2383 **worn out**

倦 Few things makes a *person* more **worn out** during the school year than having to sit an *exam paper.* [10]

2384 **model**

範 Take your mind off of catwalks and scale airplane kits and think of **model** in the sense of a pattern or example. The elements: *bamboo . . . car . . . fingerprint.* [15]

❖ **nameplate**

夗 Instead of coming home in the *evening* and fumbling with your keys to open your front door, you simply run your *fingerprint* across your backlit **nameplate** and, presto!—you're in. [5]

夕 夗

2385 **resentment**

怨 *Nameplate . . . heart.* [9]

2386 **winding** (ADJ.)

宛 *House . . . nameplate.* [8]

❖ Used as a primitive element, this character will mean *mailbox*, from the little *house* with your *nameplate* on it that the postman drops your mail into.

2387		wrist
腕	*Part of the body . . . mailbox.* [12]	

2388		tactful
婉	*Woman . . . mailbox.* [11]	

2389		bowl
碗	*Stone . . . mailbox.* [13]	

2390		deceitful
詭	*Words . . . danger.* [13]	

2391		kneel
跪	*Wooden leg . . . danger.* [13]	

2392		popular
輿	*Zipper . . . car . . . tool.* [17]	
	ﺃ 圃 圃 圃 輿	

LESSON 37

2393 酬	reward (N./V.)
	Whiskey bottle . . . state. [13]
2394 酌	pour wine
	Whiskey bottle . . . ladle. [10]
2395 酷	brutal
	Whiskey bottle . . . declare. [14]
2396 醇	mellow wine
	Whiskey bottle . . . enjoy. [15]
2397 醋	vinegar
	Whiskey bottle . . . times past. [15]
❖ 卒	foot soldiers
	The **foot soldiers** shown here are not your ordinary rank-and-file infantry, but specially manufactured, sophisticated "foot" masseurs for commanding officers. See them march off the *assembly line* in their *top hats* with foot-long *needles* in hand to prick the boils of their commanding officers. [8}

亠　众　卒

2398 醉	drunk
	Whiskey bottle . . . foot soldiers. [15]
2399 粹	unmixed
	Rice . . . foot soldiers. The key word connotes something that is pure and unadulterated. [14]

| 2400 翠 | emerald green |
| Feathers . . . foot soldiers. [14] | |

| 2401 碎 | shattered |
| Stone . . . foot soldiers. [13] | |

❖ 夋

streetwalker

You shouldn't have any trouble associating the character for *consent* and a pair of *walking legs* with a **streetwalker**. (Note that in the hand-drawn character, the *human legs* in *consent* end up looking more like a pair of *animal legs*.) [7]

厶　厷　夋

| 2402 酸 | sour |
| Whiskey bottle . . . streetwalker. [14] | |

| 2403 梭 | shuttle (N.) |
| Tree . . . streetwalker. Think back to the original **shuttle** from which things like space **shuttles**, airport **shuttles**, and even **shuttle**cocks get their names in English, namely the little piece of wood that flies back and forth over the loom. [11] | |

| 2404 峻 | lofty |
| Mountain . . . streetwalker. [10] | |

| 2405 俊 | pretty |
| Person . . . streetwalker. [9] | |

2406 釁

quarrel (N.)

This is not one of the more elegant Chinese characters. It is almost as if the primitive elements were members of a committee having a **quarrel** among themselves for the place of dominance and each insisting on its right to show up. At the top we have the *zipper* with a *hood* containing a *one* and a *spike* (driven into the element beneath it). Next comes a *crown* that covers the *whiskey bottle* and the primitive for *part*. By this time, you should have all the tools necessary to create an outlandish story to be sure that all the members of the committee are each set in the proper place. [25]

2407	thick sauce
醬	The character for **thick sauce** also appears in the term for soy sauce, so it is one you have probably seen many times already without realizing it. The primitive elements: *General . . . whiskey bottle.* [18]

2408	just like
猶	*Pack of wild dogs . . . chieftain.* [12]

2409	found (v.)
奠	The sense of the key word is to establish an institution. Its elements: *chieftain . . . St. Bernard dog.* [12]

2410	squat (v.)
蹲	*Wooden leg . . . venerate.* [19]

2411	tease (v.)
逗	*Beans . . . road.* [10]

2412	(rhetorical question)
豈	This character has no particular meaning on its own but is used to form **rhetorical questions**. The primitive elements, *mountain and beans*, suggest that compared to real questions with real answers, **rhetorical questions** don't amount to a hill of *beans*— let alone a *mountain* of them. If you turn to FRAME 1170 of Book 1, you will see that we hinted at something similar there. [10]

2413 凱	**triumphant**
	Mountain of beans . . . wind. Not to twist your story down the wrong path, but if you think of the key word as suggesting someone **triumphant** who has been "tooting his own horn," the transition from a *mountain of beans* to *wind* should be pretty simple. [12].
2414 豎	**perpendicular**
	Scrooge . . . beans. The sense of this key word is vertical or upright. [15]
2415 嘉	**commend**
	Drum . . . add. You might also want to try beginning with the character for *joyful* and simply nudge the element for *mouth* over to make room to complete the character for *add.* [14]
2416 嘻	**giggling**
	Mouth . . . joyful. [15]
2417 盟	**alliance**
	Bright . . . dish. [13]
2418 孟	**Mencius**
	This character is best known as the beginning of the name of one of ancient China's most celebrated philosophers, **Mencius** (385–303 BCE). Its primitives: *child . . . dish.* [8]
2419 猛	**fierce**
	Wild dogs . . . Mencius. [11]
2420 盛	**flourishing**
	This key word refers to something that is prospering. Its elements: *turn into . . . dish.* [11]

2421 盞	small cup Float . . . dish. [13]
2422 盒	small box Fit . . . dish. [11]
2423 盜	master thief Water . . . yawn . . . dish. [12]
2424 盪	swing (v.) Soup . . . dish. [17]
2425 寧	calm (ADJ.) House . . . heart . . . dish . . . spike. [14]
2426 盈	replete Fist . . . again . . . dish. [9]
2427 盆	basin Part . . . dish. For the particular connotation of this key word, think of a wash**basin**. [9]
2428 盃	trophy No . . . dish. [9]
2429 蘊	amass Flowers . . . thread . . . prisoner . . . dish. [20]
2430 濫	indiscriminate Water . . . hidden camera. [17]

2431	probe (v.)
鑑	*Gold . . . hidden camera.* Take this key word as meaning to delve into or investigate something. [22]

❖	Frankenbowser
尢	You will recall the primitive element for the freakish transformation of the little chihuahua into *Frankenpooch* from Book 1 (page 108). Here we see a later and no less ghastly experiment with the larger *St. Bernard dog*, something we like to call the **Frankenbowser**. [3]

ノ 尢 尢

2432	abashed
尲	*Frankenbowser . . . hidden camera.* [17]

2433	embarrassed
尬	*Frankenbowser . . . introduce.* [7]

2434	toss (v.)
抛	*Fingers . . . Frankenbowser . . . muscles.* [8]

❖	Frankenbowser Rex
尤	The transformation of the first stroke of *Frankenbowser* into a *crown* gives us the *crowning* experiment of the mad scientist: a creature that can stand shoulder to shoulder with the fiercest beasts of the Jurassic age—the **Frankenbowser Rex**. [4]

宀 尣 尤

2435	indulge in
耽	*Ear . . . Frankenbowser Rex.* [10]

2436	pillow
枕	*Tree . . . Frankenbowser Rex.* [8]

2437   view [v.]

覽

The bottom half of the character is clearly the character for *see*. The top half is the problem. At first glance, it looks very much like the character for *supervise* learned in FRAME 1080. The only difference is the substitution of a *net* in place of the *dish*. If that seems too much bother, then just work with the elements: *underling . . . reclining . . . drop of . . . net*. [21].

臣   臣   臣   臨   覽

* Used as a primitive element, this character will take the more concrete meaning of a *magnifying glass*. You might try working that into your story for the character itself.

2438   take on

攬

The sense of the key word is to **take on** a task or assume responsibility for something. Its component elements: *fingers . . . magnifying glass*. [24]

2439   cable [N.]

纜

Thread . . . magnifying glass. [27]

2440   ruthless

狠

Pack of wild dogs . . . silver. [9]

2441   hate [v.]

恨

State of mind . . . silver. [9]

2442   upper crust

爵

Vulture . . . net . . . silver . . . glued to. Europeans are not the only ones with a history of nobility, peerage, and aristocracy. China, too, had its **upper crust**. [17]

2443   chew [v.]

嚼

Mouth . . . upper crust. [20]

❖

豕

.   leopard

This primitive represents a **leopard** by combining the *claw* with the first part of the element for a *sow*. Note how the final stroke of *claw* is turned and lengthened to double up with the first stroke of *sow*.

Actually, this primitive derives from the character in FRAME 2446 just below. [7]

2444	wholeheartedly
懇	*Leopard . . . silver . . . heart.* [17]

2445	reclaim
墾	*Leopard . . . silver . . . soil.* As you may have guessed from the primitive at the bottom, this character means to **reclaim** unproductive lands for cultivation. [16]

2446	leopard
豹	*Leopard . . . ladle.* [10]

2447	cat
貓	*Leopard . . . tomato seedlings.* [16]

2448	mien
貌	*Leopard . . . dove . . . human legs.* [14]

2449	lucent
朗	*Halo . . . moon.* [10]

2450	wolf
狼	*Pack of wild dogs . . . halo.* [10]

2451 飢	*Food . . . wind.* [10]	starving
2452 饒	*Food . . . Pigpen.* [20]	spare [v.]
2453 飾	*Food . . . reclining . . . towel.* [13]	ornaments
2454 飲	*Food . . . yawn.* [12]	beverage
2455 蝕	*Food . . . insect.* [14]	eat away
2456 飽	*Food . . . wrap.* [13]	sated
2457 饅	*Food . . . mandala.* [19]	bread
2458 餅	*Food . . . puzzle.* [14]	cookie
2459 餃	*Food . . . mingle.* [14]	dumpling
2460 餓	*Food . . . miser.* [15]	hungry
2461 潛	*Water . . . two waitresses . . . sun.* [15]	submerge

2462	silkworm
蠶	This character shows two **silkworms** that have managed to escape death at the hands of the enterprising sericulturists. The *day before* they are scheduled to be boiled alive in their silk sheets, the *insects* escape into the open and fly away to begin their careers as *waitresses* at a local diner. [24]
2463	irrigate
溉	*Water . . . since.* [12]
2464	incensed
慨	*State of mind . . . since.* Be sure you put the accent of the key word on the second syllable. [12]

LESSON 38

2465

萍

duckweed

Flowers . . . water . . . water lily. The small aquatic plant known as **duckweed** gets its name from the fact that it is a culinary delicacy for ducks. [12]

艹　氵　萍

2466

秤

scale (N.)

The sense of the key word is a **scale** for weighing. The elements: *wild rice . . . water lily.* Do not confuse with the primitive of the same name. [10]

2467

淆

confuse

Water . . . sheaf . . . possess. [11]

2468

艾

Chinese mugwort

Beneath the *flowers* at the top, we see a *sheaf*, giving us a **Chinese mugwort**, one of the herbs used in the heat therapy known as moxibustion. [6]

2469

哎

Good grief!

The character expresses a mood, not fully verbalized as the key word is, of surprise at something unfortunate that has happened. Its primitives are: *mouth . . . Chinese mugwort.* [9]

2470

拔

pull out

Fingers . . . chihuahua with a *sheaf* of nettles lodged in its paw that it has to **pull out**. Pay special attention to the addition of the final stroke. [8]

扌　扌　扩　扙　拔　拔

2471	climb (v.)
攀	Woods with two sheaves . . . St. Bernard dog . . . hand. [19]

木　松　棥　樊　攀

2472	stockpile (v.)
屯	One . . . pit . . . fishhook. [4]

一　口　屯

❖ The primitive meaning of this character is *earthworm*, which is more colorful than the key word. If you think of trying to *stockpile* a shipment of *earthworms*, you should have all you need.

2473	pause (N./v.)
頓	Earthworm . . . head. [13]

2474	ton
噸	Mouth . . . pause. [16]

2475	unadulterated
純	Thread . . . earthworm. Be sure to keep this key word distinct from the character for *unmixed* (FRAME 2399); both words carry the sense of "pure." [10]

2476	fall due
屆	Flag . . . soldier in a pit. Think of things that **fall due**, like a debt with a date of expiration. [8]

2477	teeth
齒	The primitive elements of this character—*footprint . . . assembly line . . . floor . . . assembly line . . . pit*—may not be as helpful as seeing a pictograph of the top and bottom front **teeth**. [15]

止 步 歩 齿 齒

2478	shows
齣	Here we have another of those "measure words" used for counting things; in this case, the key word has to do with plays, operas, and other kinds of **shows**. Its elements: *teeth . . . sentence.* [20]

2479	length of service
齡	This key word can refer to things like one's **length of service** in the military and to the time a ship has been in use. Its elements: *teeth . . . orders.* [20]

2480	turbulent
洶	The meaning of this character can be literal or metaphorical. The elements you have to work with are: *water . . . bound up . . . sinister.* Here again, the combination of primitives on the right appeared in Book 1 (FRAME 1115). [9]

2481	fence
籬	*Bamboo . . . leave.* [24]

2482	crime
辜	*Ancient . . . chili pepper.* [12]

2483	butcher (v.)
宰	*House . . . chili pepper.* This key word means to slaughter or dress animals and also to fleece unsuspecting customers. [10]

2484	differentiate
辨	*Two chili peppers . . . saber.* [16] 辛 判 辨

2485 辮	braid (N.) Two *chili peppers . . . thread.* [20]
2486 臂	arm (N.) *Hot sauce . . . flesh.* [17]
2487 劈	split (V.) *Hot sauce . . . dagger.* [15]
2488 譬	analogy *Hot sauce . . . words.* [20]
2489 僻	out-of-the-way Picture whoever it is you chose to represent the primitive for *person* as having been secluded to an **out-of-the-way** place. As it turns out, she had been going too heavy on the *hot sauce* and the results had led to unpleasant odors coming from both ends that did not go down well in good company. [15]
❖ 睪	mermaid You catch a **mermaid** in your *net* and enjoy *good fortune* for the remainder of your days. [13] 罒 睪
2490 譯	translate *Words . . . mermaid.* [20]
2491 擇	select (V.) *Fingers . . . mermaid.* [16]
2492 澤	swamp (N.) *Water . . . mermaid.* [16]

2493	pad (N./V.)
墊	Clench . . . soil. [14]

2494	earnest
摯	Clench . . . hand. [15]

2495	entangle
糾	Thread . . . cornucopia. [8]

❖	Minute Ricemen
夌	"Listen my children and your shall hear, of the midnight ride of Paddy Revere...." The **Minute Ricemen** were an elite core of militia in the rebel army that fought for liberty from agricultural oppression during the Vegetable Rebellion of 1776 BCE. Here we see a troupe of *rice seedlings*, each fitted out with a set of *walking legs* and ready to march into battle at a minute's notice. [8]

夫 夌

2496	bully (V.)
凌	Ice . . . Minute Ricemen. [10]

2497	water caltrop
菱	Flowers . . . Minute Ricemen. [12]

2498	mausoleum
陵	Pinnacle . . . Minute Ricemen. [11]

2499	cough (V.)
咳	Mouth . . . acorn. [9]

2500	brake (V.)
剎	Sheaf . . . resin . . . saber. [9]

| 2501 嚷 | | cry out |
| Mouth . . . pigeon coop. [20] | | |

| 2502 釀 | | brew (v.) |
| Whiskey bottle . . . pigeon coop. [24] | | |

| 2503 塞 | | stronghold |
| Hamster cage . . . soil. [13] | | |

| 2504 寨 | | stockade |
| Hamster cage . . . tree. [14] | | |

LESSON 39

2505 憲	constitution The key word refers to the fundamental guiding principles of a government or other organization. Its elements: *House . . . grow up . . . eyes . . . heart.* [16]
2506 晴	sunny *Sun . . . telescope/blue or green.* [12]
2507 猜	guess *Pack of wild dogs . . . telescope.* [11]
2508 靖	pacify *Vase . . . telescope.* [13]
2509 債	debt *Person . . . responsibility.* [13]
2510 蹟	remains *Wooden leg . . . responsibility.* [18]
2511 牲	domestic animal *Cow . . . life/cell.* [9]
2512 隆	impressive *Pinnacle . . . walking legs . . . ceiling . . . cell.* [12]
2513 腥	fishy smell *Flesh . . . star.* [13]

2514 猩	orangutan *Pack of wild dogs . . . star.* [12]
2515 醒	awaken *Whiskey bottle . . . star.* [16]
2516 瞎	visionless We chose this key word to keep the character distinct from the normal word for *blind* (FRAME 458). Its elements are: *eyeballs . . . harm.* [15]
2517 轄	administer To **administer** something means to be in control of it. The difficulties begin when one is trying to **administer** more than one thing at the same time. For example, if you are doing your business on a cellphone while driving your *car* you are sure to end up doing *harm* to both tasks. [17]
2518 契	contract^(N.) *Bushes . . . dagger . . . St. Bernard dog.* [9]
2519 拜	adore Think of the key word in a religious sense. The elements: *hand . . . ceiling . . . bushes.* [9]
2520 潔	spotless *Water . . . bushes . . . dagger . . . thread.* [15]
❖ 夆	briar *féng* Think here of the hordes of would-be princes who perished on the **briar** *bushes*—or at least ended up with bloody *walking legs*—trying to make their way to Sleeping Beauty. The image of the sharply pointed **briars** will serve you well in the characters that follow. [7]

夂 冬 夆

2521	bee
蜂	*Insect . . . briar.* [13]

2522	peak [N.]
峰	*Mountain . . . briar.* [10]

2523	cutting edge
鋒	*Metal . . . briar.* This character can be used for the sharp point of an implement or for its finely honed **cutting edge**. [15]

2524	chance upon
逢	*Briar . . . road.* [10]

2525	disheveled
蓬	If it is true that the rain falls on the good and the wicked alike without discrimination, the same can be said of *flowers* blowing about in the spring breeze: they *chance upon* all heads equally, the sheveled and the **disheveled** alike. Another reason not to worry about whether your hair is combed or not. [14]

2526	sew
縫	*Thread . . . chance upon.* [16]

2527	play an instrument
奏	*Bonsai . . . heavens.* [9]

2528	gather together
湊	This key word can be used when people **gather together** as well as when people **gather together** things. The elements: *water . . . play an instrument.* [12]

2529 秦	Qin
	Bonzai . . . wild rice. **Qin** Shi Huang was the founder and first emperor of the **Qin** Dynasty. He undertook huge projects (the Great Wall, the Terra-Cotta Warriors, etc.) at the expense of many lives. Take care not to confuse this character with the one we learned in FRAME 2527. [10]

2530 蠢	foolish
	Springtime . . . insects. [21]

2531 捧	carry in both hands
	Fingers . . . proffer. [11]

2532 嘆	sigh ^(v.)
	Mouth . . . Popeye. [14]

2533 艱	arduous
	Popeye . . . silver. [17]

2534 灘	beach ^(N.)
	Water . . . difficult. Alternatively, you may read the primitive elements as *Han . . . turkey.* [22]

2535 畢	complete ^(v.)
	The easiest way to remember the writing of this character is to associate it with the character for *splendor* (FRAME 1181). Instead of beginning with *flowers*, draw a *sun*. Then, when you come to the final vertical stroke, run it all the way through the character, top to bottom. [10] 日 旦 早 昇 昌 昌 畢

2536 唾	saliva
	Mouth . . . droop. [11]

LESSON 40

2537 吟	recite
	As we have already learned characters for *poem* (FRAME 327) and *song* (FRAME 441), it is important to protect this key word with an image all its own. Its elements are the same as those in FRAME 1187; only the position has changed: *mouth . . . clock*. [7]

2538 貪	greedy
	Clock . . . shells. [11]

2539 琴	stringed instrument
	A pair of *jewels . . . clock*. [12]

2540 栗	chestnut
	Old West . . . tree. [10]

2541 潭	deep pool
	The *Old West* and *sunflower* paint for us a picture of a lonesome cowboy roaming aimlessly and daydreaming of his Daisy Belle as he plucks the petals off a *sunflower*. "She loves me, she loves me not. She loves me...." Little does he notice the *water* gathering at his feet as he stumbles and falls into a **deep pool**. Be careful to keep the right side of this character distinct from the character for "ticket" (FRAME 1194). [15]

2542 遷	resituate
	The key word has to do with changing the location of something or other. Be careful not to confuse with the character for *relocate* (FRAME 1354). The elements you have to work with are: *Old West . . . St. Bernard dog . . . fingerprint . . . road*. In line with our principle of counting strokes according to the handwritten form, note that the final element on the road is *fingerprint* and not *snakeskin* as in the printed form. [14]

西　　要　　覀　　遷

2543	overturn
覆	*Old West . . . recover.* Be sure to take this key word in its literal sense of turning something over or upsetting it. [18]

2544	flutter (v.)
飄	*Ticket . . . windstorm.* [20]

LESSON 41

2545	boss [N.]
鬧	Gate . . . goods. [17]
2546	broad
闊	Gate . . . lively. [17]
2547	close [V.]
閉	Gate . . . genie. [11]
2548	moisten
潤	Water . . . gate . . . jewel/king. [15]
2549	cabinet
閣	The key word here refers to a government **cabinet**. Its elements: *gate . . . each.* [14]
2550	put aside
擱	Fingers . . . cabinet. [17]
2551	explicate
闡	Gate . . . list. [20]
2552	peruse
閱	Gate . . . devil. [15]
2553	stuffy
悶	Take the key word in its literal sense of insufficiently ventilated or hard-to-breathe air. The primitives: *gate . . . heart.* [12]

2554		flash (v.)
閃	Gate . . . person. [10]	
2555		valve
閥	Gate . . . fell. [14]	
2556		floodgate
閘	Gate . . . radish. [13]	
2557		repudiate
闢	Gate . . . hot sauce. [21]	
2558		ash-colored
蒼	Flowers . . . storehouse. [14]	
2559		rob
搶	Fingers . . . storehouse. [13]	
2560		humble (ADJ.)
菲	Flowers . . . jail cell. [12]	
2561		lifetime
輩	Jail cell . . . car. [15]	
2562		sad
悲	Jail cell . . . heart. [12]	
2563		irresolute
徘	Queue . . . jail cell. [11]	

❖	xiān	jailbreak
韯	The two *persons* that this element begins with are actually a couple of inmates in a *jail cell* engaged in a daring **jailbreak**. A visitor had smuggled them a *halberd* hidden in a chocolate	

Wild onions or leeks

cake, which they take turns using to dig a hole in the *floor* of their cell—one standing watch while the other digs away. [17]

丷 丷 𦭝 𦭠 籤

2564 **annihilate**

殲

Bones . . . jailbreak. [21]

2565 **bamboo slip**

籤

The key word refers to pieces of *bamboo* that are used to draw lots, much the same as children use straws to see who gets the "short end of the stick." Here the **bamboo slips** are being drawn to see who gets to take part in the *jailbreak* and who has to stay behind to distract the guards. [23]

2566 **fiber**

纖

This character, which figures in compounds for different kinds of **fiber**, should be associated with the fine and delicate qualities we associate with the word. The elements you have to work with are: *thread . . . jailbreak.* [23]

2567 **gullet**

喉

Mouth . . . marquis. [12]

2568 **monkey**

猴

Pack of wild dogs . . . marquis. [12]

2569 **Korea**

韓

Mist . . . locket. [17]

2570 **disobey**

違

Locket . . . road. [12]

2571 **latitude**

緯

Thread . . . locket. The **latitude** this key word refers to is the opposite of longitude. [15]

LESSON 42

2572 竿	**pole** *Bamboo . . . clothesline.* [9]
2573 罕	**rarely** *Paper punch . . . clothesline/offend.* [7]
2574 軒	**veranda** *Car . . . clothesline.* [10]
2575 肝	**liver** *Flesh . . . offend.* [7]
2576 刊	**publication** This character refers to the finished product, not to the process of preparing it. Its elements: *clothesline . . . saber.* [5]
2577 汗	**sweat** [N.] *Water . . . offend.* [6]
2578 桿	**shaft** The *drought tree* is a special botanical wonder, found only in a certain region within the deserts of central Australia (we are sworn to secrecy on the precise location), so named because it is able to survive the periodic *droughts* that claim all other vegetation. The locals have discovered that if they carve a long **shaft** from the *tree*, it will lead them to underground wells. [11]
2579 悍	**bold** *State of mind . . . drought.* [10]

2580 徐	slowly
Queue . . . scale. [10]	

2581 敘	recount (v.)
Scale . . . taskmaster. The meaning of the key word is to narrate or give an account. [11]	

2582 塗	smear (v.)
Water . . . scale . . . soil. [13]	

2583 斜	slanting
Scale . . . Big Dipper. [11]	

2584 喇	flared horn
Mouth . . . bundle . . . saber. [12]	

2585 嗽	hack (v.)
The key word here refers to the way people cough who have been smoking so long their lungs never quite seem to clear. It has nothing to do with cutting things up or breaking into computer systems. Its elements: *mouth . . . bundle . . . yawn.* [14]	

2586 賴	rely on
Bundle . . . dagger . . . shells. [16]	

2587 懶	lazy
State of mind . . . rely on. [19]	

2588 嫩	tender (ADJ.)
Woman . . . bundle . . . taskmaster. [14]	

2589 煉	refine
You **refine** things when you submit them to *fire.* This applies to a range of things from metals to milk (when you pasteurize it).	

Here you are trying the process out on a *horned toad*, hoping the *fire* will save you the disgusting obligation of kissing it to turn it into a handsome Prince or beautiful Princess—whichever your preference. [13]

2590 錬	chain (N.)
	Gold . . . horned toad. [17]

2591 腫	swollen
	Flesh . . . heavy. [13]

2592 董	director
	Flowers . . . heavy. [13]

2593 鍾	draw together
	Metal . . . heavy. You might want to try reading these primitives in reverse order to make your image of something that can **draw together** an entire generation. [17]

2594 痰	phlegm
	Sickness . . . inflammation. [13]

2595 症	disease
	Sickness . . . correct. [10]

2596 疼	hurt (v.)
	Sickness . . . winter. [10]

2597 癒	get well
	Sickness . . . more and more. [18]

2598 疫	epidemic
	Sickness . . . missile. [9]

2599 癌	cancer
	Sickness . . . goods . . . mountain. [17]

2600 疲	fatigued
	Sickness . . . covering. [10]

2601 疾	rapid
	Be sure to keep this character distinct from *quick* (FRAME 1237). Picture a succession of poison *darts* (the sort that inflict *sickness*) flying out **rapid**-fire from a blowgun, so that "**rapid**-fire" can conjure up the proper image. [10]

2602 痴	idiotic
	Sickness . . . know. [13]

2603 **tumor**

瘤 *Sickness . . . stay.* [15]

2604 **trace** (N.)

痕 *Sickness . . . silver.* [11]

2605 **itch** (V.)

癢 *Sickness . . . raise.* [20]

2606 **paralysis**

癱 *Sickness . . . difficult.* [24]

2607 **sore** (N.)

瘡 *Sickness . . . storehouse.* [15]

❖ **Heartbreak Hotel**

㥯 The *vulture's claw* at the top and the *heart* at the bottom tells us that we have to do with an emotionally wrenching experience. Actually, this is the logo for the **Heartbreak Hotel** now "under construction" (the *I-beam*) in your neighborhood. As for the *broom*, think of it as the equipment of the staff, which has not only to clean the rooms and change the bedding, but also to sweep away all the bad karma that accumulates there. [14]

2608 **stable** (ADJ.)

穩 *Wild rice . . . Heartbreak Hotel.* [19]

2609 **hidden**

隱 *Pinnacle . . . Heartbreak Hotel.* [17]

2610 **addiction**

癮 *Sickness . . . hidden* [22]

2611

巨

gigantic

If you look at this character ignoring the order in which its strokes are written, you see a *box* with another *box* turned around and placed inside of it. In the fierce competition to hold the Guinness World Record for the world's largest *box,* someone has put the previous record holder's *box* inside a *box* so **gigantic** that it takes up an entire city block. [4]

一   ⺮   ⺕   巨

❖ In line with the key word, this character will mean a *giant* when used as a primitive. Some fairy-tale *giant* you remember from your childhood, like the one in "Jack and the Beanstalk," should do nicely.

2612

渠

canal

Water . . . giant . . . tree. [11]

2613

拒

refuse (v.)

Fingers . . . giant. [7]

2614

矩

square (n.)

Dart . . . giant. [9]

2615

距

distance

Wooden leg . . . giant. [11]

2616

框

rectangular frame

Tree . . . box . . . jewel. This character can be used in words referring to the **rectangular frames** around pictures, windows, doors, and the like. [10]

2617

筐

rectangular basket

Bamboo . . . box . . . king. Nowadays this character can be used for baskets of various shapes, but formerly it was associated with **rectangular baskets** woven of bamboo strips. [12]

竻　竺　笙　筐

2618	smash (v.)
砸	*Stone . . . box . . . towel.* [10]
2619	converge
匯	*Box . . . water . . . turkey.* [13]
2620	artisan
匠	*Box . . . tomahawk.* [6]
2621	bandit
匪	*Box . . . jail cell.* [10]
2622	keep out of sight
匿	*Box . . . Disneyland.* [11]
2623	pocket
兜	This character is composed of a *dove* flapping about between two facing *boxes*, and a pair of *human legs*. [11]

白　𡭆　𦥯　兜

2624	vomit (v.)
嘔	*Mouth . . . region.* [14]
2625	hit (v.)
毆	*Region . . . missile.* [15]
2626	human body
軀	*Somebody . . . region.* [18]

2627 昂	hold one's head high
	Sun . . . stamp collection. [8]

2628 抑	curb ^(v.)
	The sense of the key word is to restrain, as in "to **curb** one's emotions." The elements: *fingers . . . stamp collection.* [7]

2629 葵	large-flowered plants
	Flowers . . . teepee . . . heavens. [13].

❖ 尞	pup tent
	The *St. Bernard dog* and its overlap with the element for *teepee* suggest the meaning of this primitive element: a **pup tent**. The combination of *sun* and *small* at the bottom can be seen as a little opening or flap through which the *sun* shines in the morning to let you know it's time to get up. [12]

大　大　尣　呇　尞

2630 僚	coworker
	Person . . . pup tent. [14]

2631 遼	far away
	Pup tent . . . road. [15]

2632 瞭	comprehend
	Eyeball . . . pup tent. [17]

2633 療	cure ^(v.)
	It is gradually coming to dawn on medical science that it is possible to **cure** most of the *sickness* of the world in a *pup tent* with a sensible medic and a modicum of supplies, a far less expensive and far more expansive project than lugging patients off to the nearest full-service hospital. [17]

2634 瞪	Eyeball . . . stepladder. [17]	glare (v.)
2635 凳	Stepladder . . . small table. [14]	bench
2636 澄	Water . . . stepladder. [15]	transparent
2637 潑	Water . . . courier. [15]	splash (v.)
2638 撥	Fingers . . . courier. [15]	allocate

Lesson 44

2639	fir tree
杉	*Tree . . . rooster tail.* [7]

2640	well-mannered
彬	*Tree . . . fir tree.* Make sure your image of this character's key word is kept distinct from the one you have for *well-behaved* (FRAME 1677). [11]

2641	shirt
衫	*Cloak . . . rooster tail.* [8]

2642	manifest (ADJ.)
彰	*Chapter . . . rooster tail.* [14]

2643	puffy
膨	*Flesh . . . drum . . . rooster tail.* As is obvious from the primitive on the left, this character refers to the condition of being bloated or swollen, not to being pompous or running short of breath. [16]

2644	take advantage of
趁	You **take advantage of** the fine weather by leaving the bar and taking your daily *cocktail* for a *walk*. [12]

2645	diagnose
診	*Words . . . cocktail.* This key word should be taken in its medical sense. [12]

2646	seep
滲	*Water . . . drunks at a bar.* [14]

	kiddie cocktail
❖ 翏	Instead of the cutesy umbrella that usually comes with your Shirley Temple, this **kiddie cocktail** puts a not-so-cutsey pair of mechanical flapping *wings*, splattering the contents of the *cocktail* over everyone—to the delight of all the **kiddies**. [11]

羽羽　翏

2647	gum
膠	*Flesh . . . kiddie cocktail.* Think of the thick, sticky goo that oozes out of trees and plants, not the stuff you chew on and blow bubbles with before you stick it under your desk. [15]

2648	wrong (ADJ.)
謬	*Words . . . kiddie cocktail.* [18]

2649	deserted
寥	*House . . . kiddie cocktail.* [14]

2650	speck
斑	*Highlander* between two *balls.* [12]

王　玟　斑

2651	design (N.)
紋	*Thread . . . Highlander.* The sense of the key word is a pattern, like the kind you might find on your dinnerware. [10]

2652	small shovel
鏟	*Metal . . . products.* [19]

2653	Samoa
薩	This character is used phonetically in many names, including that for the country of **Samoa**, for which it provides the first character. Its elements: *flowers . . . pinnacle . . . products.* [18]

2654	backbone
脊	*Sparkler . . . person . . . flesh.* [10]

= =＝ 夬 脊

2655	letter
函	The key word for this character refers to **letters** sent in correspondence, not to the symbols of the alphabet. Its elements: *snare . . . sparkler . . . pit.* [8]

一 丅 丂 㐅 㐈 㐆 函 函

2656	culvert
涵	*Water . . . letter.* [11]

2657	reflect
映	*Sun . . . center.* The key word refers to what mirrors and shiny objects do, not to any contemplative activity. [9]

2658	calamity
殃	*Bones . . . center.* [9]

2659	plump
肥	*Flesh . . . mosaic.* [8]

2660	crawl [v.]
爬	*Claw . . . mosaic.* [8]

2661	scar [N.]
疤	*Sickness . . . mosaic.* [9]

2662	gorgeous
艷	*Plentiful . . . color.* [24]

Lesson 45

2663 甜	sugary The *tongue* that speaks *sweet* words is typical of the many things in life that can be described as **sugary**. As long as you stick to the positive connotations of the term, even your special sweetie qualifies. Note that here we have reverted to the key word meaning of the element 甘. From the following frame, we will revert to its primitive meaning. [11]
2664 鉗	pliers *Metal . . . wicker basket.* [13]
2665 媒	matchmaker *Woman . . . such and such.* [12]
2666 煤	coal *Fire . . . such and such.* [13]
2667 謀	scheme (v.) *Words . . . such and such.* [16]
2668 棋	chess *Tree . . . hamper.* [12]
2669 欺	dupe (v.) *Hamper . . . yawn.* [12]
2670 旗	flag (N.) *Banner . . . hamper.* Be sure you create an image of a **flag** as different as possible from the one you use for the primitive element of the same meaning. [14]

2671 嘶	hoarse
	Mouth . . . Sphinx. [15]

2672 撕	rip (v.)
	Fingers . . . Sphinx. [15]

❖ 甚	{1291} *shén* Hercules
	The abstract key word *tremendously* does not suggest a consistent image. We will therefore replace it with the figure of **Hercules**, remembered for his *tremendously* arduous tasks. [9]

2673 堪	tolerate
	Soil . . . Hercules. [12] *kān*

2674 勘	survey (v.)
	Hercules . . . muscle. [11]

2675 遣	dispatch (v.)
	Purse . . . maestro . . . road. [13]

2676 譴	censure (v.)
	Words . . . dispatch. Remember to draw the element for *road* in *dispatch* last. [20]

2677 囊	sack (N.)
	This character is exactly the same as the primitive for *pigeon coop*, except that a *purse* and a *crown* are tucked inside of the *top hat.* Pay attention to the opening stroke order and you will see how the fourth stroke of the *purse* is also used in drawing the *top hat*, and the last stroke doubles up with the second stroke of the *crown.* [22]

2678 潰	burst^(v.)
	Water . . . expensive. [15]

2679 櫃	cupboard
	Tree . . . box . . . expensive. [18]

2680 宜	fitting^(ADJ.)
	Take this key word in its sense of suitable or appropriate. The elements are: *house . . . shelves.* [8]

2681 誼	friendship
	Words . . . fitting. [15]

2682 租	rent^(N./V.)
	Wild rice . . . shelves. [10]

2683 粗	coarse
	Rice . . . shelves. [11]

2684 阻	block^(v.)
	Pinnacle . . . shelves. [8]

❖ 晶	think tank
	You will remember that in Lesson 2 (FRAMES 23 and 24) we noted that the triplification of a single element means "everywhere" or "heaps of" something or other. Here we have three *brains* stacked up to represent the heaps of *brains* that make up a **think tank**. [15]

田　　　田／田　　　晶

2685 疊	heap^(v.)
	Think tank . . . crown . . . shelves. [22]

2686	baseball base
壘	**Baseball bases**, of course, are used in the national sport of the United States. The elements: *think tank . . . soil*. [18].

2687	hoe ^(N./V.)
鋤	*Metal . . . assist.* [15]

LESSON 46

2688 叢	**thicket** *Side by side and upside down . . . soil . . . take.* Note the doubling up of the first stroke for *take* and the last of *soil.* [18]
❖ 業	**yoga** The reason these *husbands* are set *side by side and upside down* has to do with their **yoga** therapy for male chauvinism. [12] 業 業
2689 樸	**plain** (ADJ.) *Tree . . . yoga.* [16]
2690 撲	**pounce on** *Fingers . . . yoga.* [15]
2691 僕	**servant** *Person . . . yoga.* [14]
2692 譜	**musical score** *Words . . . universal.* [19]
2693 哄	**fool** (V.) *Mouth . . . together.* [9]
2694 洪	**deluge** Think of the **deluge** here as a great flood, not as a heavy downpour. The elements: *water . . . together.* [9]

2695 烘	warm by a fire
	Fire . . . together. [10]

2696 恭	respectful
	Together . . . valentine. [10]

2697 拱	arch ^(N./V.)
	Fingers . . . together. [9]

arch (N./V.)

2698 暴	violent
	Sun . . . together . . . snowflakes. [15]

日　異　暴

2699 瀑	waterfall
	Water . . . violent. [18]

2700 爆	explode
	Fire . . . violent. [19]

2701 殿	ceremonial hall
	Flag . . . together . . . missile. [13]

2702 戴	have on
	Chinese distinguishes between major items of clothing that people "wear" and accessories like glasses, hats, and bracelets, which they **have on**. *Thanksgiving . . . different.* [17]

土　壴　𡎛　戴

2703 翼	wings
	Wings . . . different. This is the character from which we derived the primitive of the same meaning. [17]

2704	dung
糞	*Rice . . . different.* You might want to compare the character for **dung** to the primitive for *fertilizer*. The two are similar in meaning and in drawing. [17]

2705	compose
撰	Think here of what you do when you **compose** a term paper. The primitives are: *fingers . . .* two *snakeskins . . . together.* [15]

LESSON 47

2706 啞	mute (ADJ.) *Mouth . . . Asia.* [11]
2707 壺	kettle *Soldier . . . crown . . . Asia.* Note that the second stroke of *crown* doubles up as the first stroke of *Asia* [12]
2708 蟹	crab (N.) *Untie . . . insect.* [19]
2709 懈	lax People are said to be **lax** when they are negligent of their duties. The character suggests that they are in a *state of mind* that has *untied* itself from the real world. [16]
2710 購	purchase (V.) *Shells . . . sieve.* [17]
2711 溝	ditch (N.) *Water . . . sieve.* [13]
❖ 龠	study group The *meeting* of *three mouths* gathered around a *tome* gives us a **study group.** [17] 人　龠　龠
2712 鑰	key This is the same **key** as the primitive element, so be sure not to confuse the two images. Here the elements are: *gold . . . study group.* [25]

2713 籲	plead
	Bamboo . . . study group . . . page. [32]

2714 冊	Vol.
	This character is similar to the primitive for *tome* learned in Book 1 (page 344), except that the stroke order is different and the final stroke extends on both ends. [5]

$$)\quad 刀\quad 刖\quad 冊\quad 冊$$

2715 刪	delete
	Vol. . . . saber. [7]

2716 柵	palisade
	Here we have a very special **Palisade** Park. Now a **palisade** fence is usually made of stakes driven into the ground, but here it is made of *trees* lined up and joined to one another by one of the *Vols.* of an encyclopedia spread open and attached to a trunk on each side. That way, when people stop for a rest on their walk through **Palisade** Park, they can not only enjoy the shade of the *tree* but further their education at the same time. [9]

2717 珊	coral
	Ball . . . Vol. [9]

2718 遍	everywhere
	Book cover . . . road. [12]

2719 偏	partial
	Person . . . book cover. The sense of the key word is that of having a bias or preference for someone or something. [11]

2720 淪	sink (v.)
	Water . . . library. [11]

2721	human relationships
倫	*Person . . . library.* [10]

LESSON 48

2722 抵	resist *Fingers . . . calling card.* [8]
2723 㟃	hoodlum *Deceased . . . people.* [8]
2724 哺	breastfeed *Mouth . . . dog tag.* [10]
2725 鋪	shop ^(N.) *Metal . . . dog tag.* [15]
2726 輔	supplement ^(V.) *Car . . . dog tag.* [14]
2727 捕	capture *Fingers . . . dog tag.* [10]
2728 敷	apply *Dog tag . . . release.* This key word refers to what you do when you slap on powders, ointments, and other things. Also, step back to FRAME 1701 to remind yourself of how the left half of the element for *release* gets compressed. [15]
2729 浦	river mouth *Water . . . dog tag.* [10]
2730 蒲	cattail Conveniently, **cattails** are found in the wetlands and around *river mouths.* Think of the furry *flowers* of the **cattails** as belong-

ing to actual cats submerged under the water, and watch what happens when you try to pull one up! [14]

2731

薄

slight (ADJ.)

The character for **slight** needs an image of something thin and frail: like a *cattail glued to* the hindquarters of your pet Siamese, who lost hers in an alley brawl. [17]

2732

簿

register (N.)

Bamboo . . . water . . . gummed label. [19]

2733

傅

mentor

Person . . . gummed label. [12]

2734

縛

bind fast

Thread . . . gummed label. [16]

2735

郭

outer walls

Enjoy . . . city walls. This is the character on which the primitive meaning *city walls* is based. [11]

2736

廓

limitless

Cave . . . outer walls. [14]

2737

鄙

despicable

Mouth . . . top hat . . . return . . . city walls. [14]

2738

耶

Jerusalem

Once again, we beg your leave to introduce a key word that draws on the largely phonetic value of a character. In this case, it is the first of four characters used in the transliteration for the city **Jerusalem**. Its elements are *ear . . . city walls.* [9]

2739

爺

grandfather

Father . . . Jerusalem. [13]

2740	outskirts
郊	*Mingle . . . city walls.* The key word refers to the area outlying a major city, both suburbs as well as the countryside. [9]

2741	nation
邦	The *bushes* that appear on the left here are bent because they were planted too close to the *city walls* and cannot grow naturally. All in all, not a bad metaphor for what happens to a **nation** when it closes itself in against the outside world as if it were a fortress that needed guarding. If the *city walls* were torn down, not only would the *bushes* grow straight, the people inside would be able to enjoy them. [7]

2742	truss (v.)
綁	*Thread . . . nation.* [13]

2743	post (v.)
郵	*Droop . . . city walls.* The key word connotes what you do when you drop a letter into the mailbox. [11]

2744	Deng
鄧	*Stepladder . . . city walls.* This key word is the family name of **Deng** Xiaoping, a famous leader of the Chinese Communist Party. Known as the architect of "socialism with Chinese characteristics," he led China into what is called a "socialist market economy." [15]

2745	hurl
擲	*Fingers . . . found . . . city walls.* [18]

2746	hallway
廊	*Cave . . . young man.* [12]

2747	hug (v.)
擁	*Fingers . . . top hat . . . floss . . . turkey.* [16]

2748	satin
緞	*Thread . . . section.* [15]

2749	wily
⁊	The elements, in the order of writing, are: *clothes hanger . . . drop of.* Note that the *drop* is drawn lower-left to upper-right, much like the second stroke in the primitive for "ice." [2]

2750	hold in the mouth
叼	*Mouth . . . wily.* [5]

2751	ardent
殷	*Drag . . . sun . . . clothes hanger . . . missile.* As unfamiliar as the left side of this character looks, if you draw it in the order of the primitives, it is really quite simple. [10]

丿　尸　舟　殷

2752	longevity
壽	The character for **longevity** is aptly named. At first glance, it seems as if it would take you a lifetime to learn how to write it. But break it up into its component elements and the only real work left is to combine them into a memorable image: *Soldier . . .* flattened out *clothes hanger . . . I-beam . . . one . . . inch.* [14]

土　 圭　 圭　 圭　 喜　 壽

❖ The meaning of the character will change to a *long, gray beard* when it is used as a primitive element.

2753	large waves
濤	*Water . . . long, gray beard.* [17]

2754 鑄	cast [v.]
	Aside from giving it a shape, another reason to **cast** *metal* is to give it a longer life. In this case, the proof lies in the *long, gray beard* a particular piece of *metal* is sporting. [22]

2755 禱	pray
	Altar . . . long, gray beard. [18]

2756 籌	make arrangements
	Bamboo . . . long, gray beard. [20]

2757 伺	attend to
	Person . . . take charge of. The key word connotes to serve or wait upon, not to pay attention to. [7]

2758 飼	rear [v.]
	Food . . . take charge of. The key word refers to what you do when you raise animals. [13]

2759 舶	liner
	The type of *boat* connoted by this key word is a large ocean-going **liner**. The important thing here is to work with the elements *boat* and *dove* to make a distinct image from other kinds of boats and ships. [11]

2760 航	navigate
	Boat . . . whirlwind. [10]

2761 艇	light boat
	Boat . . . royal court. [13]

2762 艦	warship
	Boat . . . supervise. [20]

2763	ship's cabin
艙	Boat . . . storehouse. [16]

2764	along (PREP.)
沿	Water . . . belch. The key word is used in phrases such as "**along the beach**." [8]

2765	lead (N.)
鉛	Words . . . belch [12]

2766	fox
狐	Pack of wild dogs . . . melon. [8]

2767	petal
瓣	Two *chili peppers* . . . melon. [19]

辛　䒑　瓣

2768 溢	**brim over**
	Water . . . benefit. Avoid using the image you had for *overflow* (FRAME 676), although the meaning is basically the same. [13]

2769 暇	**spare time**
	Day . . . braces. [13]

2770 霞	**red sky**
	As that bit of folk wisdom about the *weather* goes, "**Red sky** at night—sailor's delight; **red sky** in the morning—sailor's warning." What about the day? Just because no one has ever seen a **red sky** in the daytime is no reason not to have a proverb about it. We'll get you started and you can finish it as you wish: "**Red sky** in the day—your *braces.*. . . [17]

❖ 气	**gas**
	This primitive actually appeared twice in Book 1 (FRAMES 1360 and 1361), where it could have been introduced. Use those characters to help remember its meaning: **gas** (as opposed to a solid or liquid). [4]

$$ノ \quad ⻠ \quad 气$$

2771 氧	**oxygen**
	Gas . . . sheep. [10]

2772 氛	**atmosphere**
	Gas . . . part. [8]

2773 氯	**chlorine**
	Gas . . . snowman. [12]

2774 氫	*Gas . . . spool.* [11]	hydrogen
2775 鞏	*I-Beam . . . ordinary . . . leather.* [15]	strengthen
2776 霸	*Rain . . . leather . . . flesh.* [21]	tyrant
2777 壩	*Soil . . . tyrant.* [24]	dam (N.)
2778 勒	*Leather . . . muscles.* [11]	tighten
2779 鞠	*Leather . . . bind up . . . rice.* [17]	bow respectfully
2780 靴	*Leather . . . transform.* [13]	boots
2781 鞭	*Leather . . . convenient.* [18]	whip (N./V.)

2782 芽	sprout (N.) *Flowers . . . tusk.* Be careful not to confuse this character with the primitive of the same meaning we learned in Book 1. [8]
2783 訝	surprised *Words . . . tusk.* [11]
2784 撑	prop up *Fingers . . . outhouse . . . tooth.* [15]
2785 雅	polished The key word **polished** describes persons who are cultured or sophisticated. The elements: *tusk . . . turkey.* [12]
2786 邪	wicked *Tusk . . . city walls.* [7]
2787 奥	of great depth *Drop of . . . helmet . . . droppings . . . St. Bernard dog.* Consult FRAME 178 in Book 1 for help with combining the first two primitives. [13] 冖 奧
2788 澳	deep inlet *Water . . . of great depth.* [16]
2789 懊	remorseful *State of mind . . . of great depth.* [16]

2790	be informed
悉	*Droppings . . . heart.* [11]

2791	pilfer
竊	*Hole . . . droppings . . . magic wand . . . prisoner . . . glass cover . . . elbow.* Note that the last stroke of *prisoner* doubles up with the second stroke of *glass cover.* [22]

2792	painstaking
審	*House . . . fertilizer.* [15]

2793	auntie
嬸	*Woman . . . painstaking.* [18]

2794	blanket [N.]
毯	*Fur . . . inflammation.* [12]

2795	milli-
毫	*Tiara . . . fur.* This character features in words like **millimeter**, **milligram**, and **millisecond**. [11]

❖	Christmas tree
耒	The first stroke of this character, the *ceiling*, cuts into the element for *not yet* because the **Christmas tree** you brought home to decorate turned out to be too large for the living room and was *not yet* ready to be decorated. So you cut a hole in the *ceiling* and let the top protrude out of the floor of the upstairs bedroom. Too bad the angel won't be able to look down on the lights and tinsel this year. [6] 一　耒

2796	consume
耗	*Christmas tree . . . fur.* [10]

2797 耕	till ^(v.) *Christmas tree . . . well.* [10]
2798 籍	records *Bamboo . . . Christmas tree . . . times past.* The key word refers to official documents or registries. [20]
2799 藉	excuse ^(N.) *Flowers . . . Christmas tree . . . times past.* [18]
2800 托	hold up *Fingers . . . . fur ball.* This character has nothing to do with robbing a stagecoach or a convenience store. It refers to what you do when you **hold** something **up**, usually with one hand, palm facing upward. [6]
2801 畏	be afraid of *Brains . . . barrette.* [9]
2802 喂	Hello… *Mouth . . . be afraid of.* For reasons we can only imagine, Chinese has combined these elements into the word one uses in answering the telephone. [12]
2803 脹	bloated *Flesh . . . long.* [12]
2804 帳	tent *Towel . . . long.* [11]
2805 肆	IV As we already saw in FRAME 2117, Chinese uses special characters to avoid fraud in financial documents. The character in this frame takes the place of the usual character for *four* in that capacity. Its primitive elements: *long . . . brush.* [13]

2806   beard

鬍

Hair . . . recklessly. When drawing, write the entire top element first, and then the bottom one. [19]

髟 鬍

2807   loose

鬆

Hair . . . pine tree. [18]

髟 鬆

LESSON 52

2808	roc
鵬	The **roc**, the mythical *bird* of prey so large that it could destroy the ship of Sinbad the Sailor, only wreaks destruction because it cannot find a suitable *companion*. Where are the *bird* psychologists when you need them? [19]

2809	twitter (v.)
鳴	*Mouth . . . bird.* As the elements make obvious, this character literally means to make *bird* sounds. [14]

2810	swan
鴻	*Yangtse . . . bird.* [17]

2811	pigeon
鴿	*Fit . . . bird.* [17]

2812	crane
鶴	The **crane** is distinguished from the rest of the *birds* in the *turkey house* because it is the one that is always "craning" its neck out the top and looking around to tell the short-necked fowl what is going on elsewhere in the barnyard. [21]

2813	oriole
鶯	*Firehouse . . . bird.* [21]

2814	magpie
鵲	*Times past . . . bird.* [19]

2815	gull
鷗	*Region . . . bird.* [22]

2816 鴉	**raven** *Tusk . . . bird.* Scientific classifications aside, in ordinary usage the difference between the **raven** and the *crow* two frames below is that the former tends to sound more literary. [15]
2817 鵝	**goose** As it turns out, this character is the "fowl" half of the compound for Mother **Goose**. Its primitive elements: *miser . . . bird.* [18]
2818 烏	**crow** The only thing that distinguishes this character from that for *bird* is the omission of the one stroke that would make it *white*. Which is logical enough if you consider that there are no **crows** of that color. [10]
2819 嗚	**zoom-zoom** Of all the different sounds this character can represent onomatopoeically, we have chosen that of an automobile racing past. Or maybe a turbo-powered roadrunner. Its component elements are: *mouth . . . crow.* [13]
2820 搗	**pound with a pestle** You usually **pound with a pestle** to mix herbs into a medicine, but here your *fingers* are used to mash and grind a more challenging concoction: an entire *island.* [13]
2821 寓	**residence** *House . . . Talking Cricket.* [12]
2822 愚	**pea-brained** *Talking Cricket . . . heart.* [13]
2823 偶	**by chance** *Person . . . Talking Cricket.* [11]

2824 厲	stern
	Cliff . . . Great Wall of China. [15]

2825 勵	encourage
	Stern . . . power. [17]

2826 鋼	steel
	Gold . . . ridge of a hill. [16]

2827 崗	hillock
	Mountain . . . ridge of a hill. [11]

2828 綱	guidelines
	Thread . . . ridge of a hill. [14]

2829 逆	go against
	Note how the *mountain goat* in this character has a long tail (or, if you will, a rear-end goatee). The *mountain goat* in this character rebels at the idea of being driven to the farm. Everything in its nature **goes against** leaving the rocky hills where it feels at home. [9]

2830 溯	go upstream
	Water . . . mountain goat with a long tail *. . . moon.* A secondary sense of this character's key word is to trace something back to its origins. [13]

2831 塑	plastic (N.)
	Mountain goat with a long tail *. . . moon . . . soil.* [13]

2832 缸	vat
	Tin can . . . I-beam. [9]

2833		jar

罐

Tin can . . . stork. This is the character from which we derived our rather more modern primitive meaning of a *tin can*. [24]

		salt shaker

鹵

Usually one puts a few grains of rice into a **salt shaker** to keep the ingredients from clogging up in humid weather. Here we have an entire *sheaf* of grain *pent in* to the glass **salt shaker**. The *magic wand* at the top is there for one special purpose: when you pull it off and tap on the **salt shaker**, the lid pops off and the contents change to *Epsom salts*. [11]

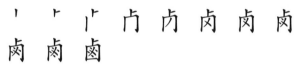

2834		depressed

鬱

A *tin can* that has been dropped and crushed in the *woods* starts us off on the character for **depressed**. Someone *sitting on the ground* next to it has good reason to be as **depressed** as the *tin can*. He has a *rooster tail* and is wearing a *crown* filled with *Epsom salts*. We leave it to your fairy-tale imagination to figure out how this all came to be. [20]

2835		salt [N.]

鹽

Supervise . . . salt shaker. Note that the *salt shaker*—which has here taken over the job of *supervising* the distribution of **salt** on your plate—takes the place of the *drop* in the character for *supervise*. [24]

2836		salty

鹹

Salt shaker . . . everybody. [20]

❖ 缶	A *bound up tin can* gives us a **canteen**. [8] ㄅ 缶	canteen

2837 掏	*Fingers . . . canteen.* [11]	draw out

2838 淘	*Water . . . canteen.* [11]	wash in a container

2839 陶	*Pinnacle . . . canteen.* [11]	pottery

2840 謠	*Words . . . canned meat.* [17]	rumor

2841 冤	*Crown . . . rabbit.* [10]	injustice

2842 饞	As complex as this character looks, a little ingenuity should simplify matters. Let the key word represent a **gluttonous** creature like the infamous gastropod Jabba the Hutt. The *food* primitive suggest an image of him at mealtime, except that here he is starting on a diet. His *mouth* is *bound up* with wire leaving only enough space for a Hutt-sized straw, which would be just large enough for a small bunny *rabbit* to pass through. Watch Jabba as he picks up the *rabbits* one by one, *compares* them with the width of the straw, and if they fit, sucks them in. [25]	gluttonous

2843 挽	*Fingers . . . hare.* [10]	tow (v.)

2844		strive
勉	Hare . . . muscle. [9]	
2845		rubber tree
橡	Tree . . . elephant. [16]	
2846		pleased
豫	Bestow . . . elephant. [16]	

LESSON 53

2847 騰	take flight Think of the key word in the sense of something that soars rapidly upward or takes a leap, like the price of a stock or the ascent of an airplane as it **takes flight**. Its elements: *flesh . . . quarter . . . horse.* [20]
2848 碼	numeral *Stone . . . horse.* The key word refers to all sorts of numerals—phone numbers, page numbers, and so forth. [15]
2849 馴	tame ^(ADJ./V.) *Horse . . . stream.* [13]
2850 瑪	Mary *Jewel . . . horse.* We choose the name **Mary** as a key word because this character is frequently used for its phonetic value in proper names like **Mary**. [14]
2851 駐	be stationed *Horse . . . candlestick.* [15]
2852 驕	arrogant *Horse . . . angel.* [22]
2853 馳	gallop ^(v.) *Horse . . . scorpion.* [13]
2854 螞	leech-hopper To the best of our knowledge, no **leech-hopper** has ever been found in nature, so you will just have to invent one to capture the sense of this key word, which is used in compounds for

various insects like locusts, dragonflies, ants, and, of course, leeches and grasshoppers. Its elements: *insect . . . horse.* [16]

2855

憑 **proof**

Ice . . . horse . . . heart. The key word refers to evidence, not to alcohol content. [16]

2856

駛 **maneuver** (v.)

Horse . . . history. One who operates vehicles like ships or planes is said to **maneuver** them. [15]

2857

騷 **disturb**

Note the drawing order and the extra drop. Then think of a carnivorous *insect* clinging to the underbelly of a *horse*, sticking in a *fork*, and gouging out little bits of supper one *drop* at a time. Picture it sitting at a little table, with a bib on, a glass of wine in hand, and a "Do not **disturb**" sign hanging alongside. [20]

馬　駁　馭　騷

2858

駕 **drive** (v.)

Add . . . horse. [15]

2859

騾 **mule**

Horse . . . tired. [21]

2860

駁 **refute**

Horse . . . two sheaves. [14]

2861

闖 **rush** (v.)

Gate . . . horse. This key word means to charge at or storm a barrier. [18]

2862

驅 **drive away**

Horse . . . region. [21]

2863		cheat [v.]
騙	*Horse . . . book cover.* [19]	

2864		trot [v.]
驟	Think here of the Hambletonian Stakes, that prestigious harness race in which the *horses* that *assemble* for the occasion, **trot**, pulling drivers riding in open, two-wheeled sulkies. [24]	

2865		hand over
遞	*Drag . . . tiger . . . road.* Note that the *tiger* takes its full form here, not its abbreviated form. [13]	

厂　虎　遞

2866		take captive
虜	*Tiger . . . male.* The reason that the third stroke in the primitive for *male* sticks out on both sides is that the *brains* of the hapless victim are hanging out both sides of the *tiger's* mouth. By the way, the stroke order for *brains* is exactly the same as you learned it before. [13]	

2867		despotic
虐	*Tiger . . . backward broom.* [9]	

虍　虍　虐　虐

2868		skin [n.]
膚	*Tiger . . . stomach.* [15]	

2869		Louvre
盧	This character, used in the phonetic transcription of the Musée du **Louvre** in Paris, shows a *tiger* eating a *dish* full of *brains.* Not a very good advertisement for tourists, especially with the guardian lions in the **Louvre** courtyard. [16]	

盧 膚 盧

| 2870 爐 | stove |
| Fire . . . . Louvre. [20] | |

| 2871 蘆 | reeds |
| Flowers . . . Louvre. [20] | |

| 2872 驢 | donkey |
| Horse . . . Louvre. [26] | |

| ❖ 丂 | snake hook |
The *snare* with an extra horizontal line gives us a **snake hook**, a *snare* at the end of a long pole used to restrain dangerous reptiles. [3]

丂 丂

| 2873 虧 | loss |
| Tiger . . . turkey . . . snake hook. [17] | |

| 2874 污 | filthy |
| Water . . . snake hook. [6] | |

| 2875 愕 | stunned |
| State of mind . . . chatterbox . . . snake hook. [12] | |

| ❖ 夸 | blowhard |
The **blowhard** tells tall tales of his safaris in the Alps where he hunted the ferocious, man-eating *St. Bernard dog* with only a **snake hook**, carving a trail through the fields of alfalfa and braving hordes of contented Swiss brown cows. [6]

大 夸

2876	brag
誇	*Words . . . blowhard.* [13]

2877	collapse ^(v.)
垮	*Soil . . . blowhard.* [9]

2878	straddle ^(v.)
跨	*Wooden leg . . . blowhard.* [13]

❖

cauldron

鬲

This is going to be a rather unusual **cauldron**. Beginning from the bottom of the primitive, we see a sturdy *spike* driven into the ground (and hence hiding the "hook" at the end) to serve as a stand for the **cauldron** to rest on. Above is a pair of *animal legs* that are attached to the bottom of the vessel as two of its "legs." The whole thing sits under a large *glass cover* that functions as a steamer lid. Oh, yes, and that *one mouth* refers to the tiny little opening at the top for letting the steam escape—like you might imagine in an ancient pressure cooker.

Note that in the hand-drawn form, the *human legs* are in fact drawn as *animal legs*, as we indicated in the little story above. This is not the first time we have met with this anomaly. [10]

一　　口　　弓　　帚　　帚　　鬲

2879	donate
獻	*Tiger . . . cauldron . . . chihuahua.* [20]

2880	melt
融	*Cauldron . . . insect.* [16]

2881	separate ^(v.)
隔	*Pinnacle . . . cauldron.* [13]

2882 濾	filter (v.)
	Water . . . ponder. [18]

2883 慶	celebrate
	Deer . . . flattened out clothes hanger . . . heart . . . walking legs. You may recall that the combination of elements below the *deer* appeared twice before, in Book 1 (FRAMES 542 and 762). [15]

2884 薦	recommend
	Flowers . . . deer . . . slingshot . . . dovetail. Note the doubling up in these last two elements. [17]

❖ 舛	sunglasses
	The element for *evening* adds a second lens to our *monocle,* giving us *sunglasses,* whose function is, after all, to darken the daylight. [6]

丿　ク　タ　タ　夗　舛

2885 傑	outstanding
	Person . . . sunglasses . . . tree. [13]

2886 瞬	instant
	Eyeball . . . vulture . . . crown . . . sunglasses. [17]

❖ 粦	jack-o'-lantern
	Picture a pumpkin at night with *rice* spurting out the top like an eruption of fireworks. The *sunglasses* show that it not just your ordinary run-of-the-mill Halloween pumpkin, but belongs to the fashionable **jack-o'-lantern** set. [12]

米　粦

2887 麟	Chinese unicorn *Deer . . . jack-o'-lantern.* Obviously, the **Chinese** idea of a **unicorn** is very different from the European one. [23]
2888 憐	pity^(v.) *State of mind . . . jack-o'-lantern.* [15]
2889 鄰	neighbor *Jack-o'-lantern . . . city walls.* [15]
2890 曬	bask To **bask** in the *sun* was long thought to make one more *lovely*. Little did they know that it also increased one's chances of contracting skin cancer. [23]
2891 灑	spill^(v.) *Water . . . lovely.* [22]
2892 罷	cease *Net . . . ability.* [15]
2893 擺	put in order *Fingers . . . cease.* [18]

LESSON 54

2894 唇	Sign of the dragon . . . mouth. [10]	lips
2895 辱	Sign of the dragon . . . glue. [10]	disgrace [N./V.]
2896 震	Weather . . . sign of the dragon. [15]	quake [V.]
2897 振	Fingers . . . sign of the dragon. [10]	vibrate
2898 魄	White . . . ghost. [15]	vigor
2899 槐	Tree . . . ghost. [14]	scholar tree
2900 魅	Ghost . . . not yet. [15]	enchant
2901 瑰	Jewel . . . ghost. [14]	marvelous
2902 魂	Rising cloud . . . ghost. [14]	soul
2903 愧	State of mind . . . ghost. [13]	ashamed

2904	leader
魁	Ghost . . . Big Dipper. [14]

2905	ugly
醜	Whiskey bottle . . . ghost. [17]

2906	raised path between fields
壟	One way to keep your *land* marked off from your neighbor's is to build a **raised path between fields** that serves as a kind of natural fence. Another way, is to have a *dragon* sit on the border. "Good fences make good neighbors," as Robert Frost observed, but fearsome *dragons* probably make for even better neighbors. (This character appears frequently in terms related to monopolizing, which suggests an altogether different role for the *dragon*.) [19]

2907	dote on
寵	If people typically **dote on** their pet dogs and cats for fear they might turn against them, imagine how careful you would have to be with a *house dragon*. [19]

2908	huge
龐	Cave . . . dragon. [19]

2909	draw near
攏	Fingers . . . dragon. [19]

2910	deaf
聾	Dragon . . . ear. [22]

2911	cage (N.)
籠	Bamboo . . . dragon. Be sure to come up with an image for **cage** that does not conflict with the element for *hamster cage* we learned in Book 1. [22]

LESSON 55

2912	insert (v.)
插	Fingers . . . thousand . . . mortar. [12]
	扌　扦　插

2913	ruin (v.)
毀	Mortar . . . soil . . . missile. [13]
	臼　臼　毀

2914	mother's brother
舅	Mortar . . . male. [13]

2915	stake (N.)
椿	Tree . . . bonsai . . . mortar. As the primitive on the left suggests, this key word refers to the kind of **stake** you drive into the ground. [15]

2916	bore a hole
鑿	Side by side and upside down . . . needle . . . mortar . . . missile . . . metal. Take special care in drawing this character. It is actually a lot simpler than it seems before you start breaking it up into its component parts. [28]
	丵　丵　鑿　鑿　鑿

2917	mouse
鼠	The *mortar* at the top tells us that this **mouse** has a very peculiar looking head. The rest of its body uses a new combination of pieces we met before. Look closely and you will see a pair of *plows* at the bottom, with the "*rain*drops" from the element for

rain hanging on them, and a *fishhook* for a tail. This is a fun, if unusual character to write, so take your time combining the elements into a memorable image. [13]

臼 臼 臼 臼 臼 鼠

2918   **scurry**

鼠   *Hole . . . mouse.* [18]

❖   **mouse hairs**

鼠   The transition from "mouse" to **mouse hairs** only entails the addition of the primitive for *flood* at the top—and what could be more gruesome than a *flood* of **mouse hairs**!—and the abbreviation of the "mortar" into a *sheaf* in the critter's *mouth*. [15]

〈〈〈   㿼   鼠

2919   **dried meat**

臘   *Flesh . . . mouse hairs.* [19]

2920   **wax** (N.)

蠟   *Insect . . . mouse hairs.* [21]

2921   **hunt** (V.)

獵   *Pack of wild dogs . . . mouse hairs.* [18]

❖   **cake mixer**

叟   Here we see a labor-intensive **cake mixer**: someone sitting down with a large wooden *mortar* resting in the *crotch* of the legs, pounding away at the batter with a *walking stick*. When you use this element, you may, of course, think of a more modern, electric apparatus. [9]

′ 𠂉 𠂋 𠂋7 𠂋7 臼 申 叟

2922	vessels
艘	This character is a classifier for boats and ships. Its elements: *boat . . . cake mixer.* [15]

2923	elder brother's wife
嫂	*Woman . . . cake mixer.* [12]

2924	emaciated
瘦	*Sickness . . . cake mixer.* [14]

2925	search (v.)
搜	*Fingers . . . cake mixer.* [12]

❖	scoop
臽	Think of an ice-cream **scoop** or something similar to combine the ingredients: a *claw* and a *mortar.* [10]

爫 臼

2926	unhulled rice
稻	*Wild rice . . . scoop.* [15]

2927	tread (v.)
蹈	*Wooden leg . . . scoop.* [17]

2928	surging
滔	*Water . . . scoop.* [13]

❖	pothole
臽	When you stop to think about it, a **pothole** is a kind of *mortar* recessed in the middle of a roadway. And, as usually happens to a **pothole** when the road workers are patching it up, it is roped off—or *bound up*—with a little fence and a sign that reads "persons working." [8]

ㄅ 臽

2929 陷	get stuck

Pinnacle . . . pothole. [11]

| 2930 焰 | flame ^(N.) |

Think of a solitary **flame** here, the bigger the better, to avoid confusing this character with the simple primitive for *flames* learned in Book 1. Its elements: *fire . . . pothole.* [12]

| 2931 餡 | filling |

The key word for this character refers to the kind of **filling** you put in pies, dumplings, and steamed buns. Its elements: *food . . . pothole.* [16]

| 2932 輌 | vehicles |

This character is a measure word for counting cars. Its elements: *car/vehicle . . . yoke.* [15]

| 2933 瞞 | dissemble |

The sense of this key word is "to hide the truth from." Its elements: *eyeball . . . yoke.* [16]

| 2934 爽 | frank ^(ADJ.) |

St. Bernard dog . . . stitching. You may find the stroke order a little unusual. And you needn't worry about our fluffy friend the *St. Bernard* being sewn up into frankfurter meat. The **frank** of this key word simply means "straightforward." [11]

一　爻　爻爻　爽　爽

| 2935 綴 | embellish |

The *threads* attached to the end of the *stitching* are a fringe-like adornment to further **embellish** the finished product. Note how the four "stitches" are drawn in a different order from that of the previous frame. [14]

糹 糾 綴 綴 綴

2936	bump (v.)
碰	Stone . . . animal horns . . . saguaro cactus. You will recall from Book 1 where the primitive was first introduced that animal horns can never be left "hanging" but have always to be attached to something. [14]

2937	transfer (v.)
挪	One economical way to **transfer** hardened criminals to Alcatraz is to dangle them finger-cuffed over a long wire attached on one end to the Bay Bridge, and on the other to the dreaded island. Just slide them across San Francisco Bay to the fate that awaits them. [10]

2938	charge falsely
誣	Words . . . witch. [14]

2939	reputation
譽	Offer . . . words. [20]

2940	islet
嶼	Mountain . . . offer. [16]

2941	thick-headed
傻	Take your time with this character to be sure you have all the elements related to one another: person . . . Farmer's Almanac . . . animal legs . . . walking legs. [13]

亻 佀 俀 傻

2942	brick
磚	Stone . . . specialty. Be sure to make an image that keeps this key word distinct from the primitive of the same meaning. [16]

2943 惠	favor^(N.)

The act of kindness we refer to as a **favor** leads us back to *frame 1468* in Book 1 where we met the cluster of eight strokes at the top as an *oriental ladybug*. Just add the *heart* and the work is done. We give the drawing again here for your reference—and, of course, as a **favor**. [12]

一　曰　申　車　甫　惠

2944 穗	ear of grain

Wild rice . . . favor [17]

❖ 廣	{1473}　　　Internet

The primitive meaning of **Internet** immediately comes to mind when you think of the key word *extensive*. You may, of course, choose to retain the key-word meaning in the three frames that follow. [15]

2945 曠	expansive

Sun . . . Internet. The key word can be used for both spaces and personalities. [19]

2946 礦	mine^(N.)

Stone . . . Internet. [20]

2947 擴	enlarge

Fingers . . . Internet. [18]

2948 聰	smart

We already met the combination of the GPS and *heart* in FRAME 1476. Here it suggests something wired into the anatomy of birds to give them their extraordinary sense of direction and make them **smart** in a way our poor human IQs will never be able to emulate. Be sure to include the wiring from the GPS-equipped *heart* to the *ear* so that the voice can be heard advising, "In 200 feet turn left at the traffic light." [17]

2949 蔥	onion
	The **onion** also has its GPS-equipped *heart*, but the **onion's** *flower* has no way of knowing that fact, which may explain why they tend to stay close to home. [15]

2950 膽	gall bladder
	Flesh . . . snitch. [17]

2951 瞻	look upward
	Eyeballs . . . snitch. [18]

2952 摟	cuddle
	Fingers . . . Flying Dutchman. [14]

2953 屢	time and again
	Flag . . . Flying Dutchman. [14]

2954 濁	turbid
	Water . . . butterfly net. [16]

2955 燭	candle
	Fire . . . butterfly net. [17]

2956 觸	touch (v.)
	Safe . . . butterfly net. The sense of this key word is to bring the skin into contact with something. [20]

2957 囑	admonish
	Mouth . . . belong to. [24]

2958 欄	railing
	Tree . . . gargoyle. [21]

2959	impede
攔	*Fingers . . . gargoyle.* [20]

2960	tracks
蹤	Few **tracks** are easier to *follow* than those of someone sporting a *wooden leg*. For the **tracks** of trains and trolleys, you are better off with the character in FRAME 1597. [18]

2961	shrug (v.)
聳	*Follow . . . ear.* [17]

2962	pharmaceutical (N.)
劑	When you think of the key word **pharmaceutical**, you think of chemical compounds used as medicines (though the key word is broader in scope). Now in China, as in the West, one of the oldest principles behind the mixtures was "homeopathic," that is, the idea that the medication should be "similar" to the malady. This includes medicines in all forms and chemical agents and mixtures of many kinds—a kind of *mirror image*. All you need do is imagine the pharmacist cutting up his herbs with a long shining *saber* and you have the complete picture for a **pharmaceutical**. [16]

2963	abstain from food
齋	*Mirror image . . . small.* [17]

2964	squeeze (v.)
擠	*Fingers . . . mirror image.* [17]

2965	push button (N.)
鈕	*Metal . . . clown.* [12]

2966	shy
羞	*Wool . . . clown.* Remember how the handwritten form of the primitive for *wool* differs from the printed form. Check Index I to confirm that you have drawn it correctly. [11]

2967 紐	New York
	As we saw with the character to which we assigned the key word *L.A.* in Book 1, this character is the first in the compound for **New York**. Its primitive elements: *thread . . . clown.* [10]

2968 脾	spleen
	As in the Western tradition where the **spleen** produces black bile or "melancholy," one of the four basic bodily "humors" that affect one's temperament, in Chinese, too, this character is often associated with ill temper. Its component elements: *part of the body . . . lowly.* [12]

2969 啤	beer
	Mouth . . . lowly. This is the character that is followed by the generic character for "liquor" (see FRAME 1061) to give the term for **beer**. [11]

2970 碑	stele
	Stone . . . lowly. [13]

2971 赫	illustrious
	Crimson . . . crimson. [14]

2972 嚇	terrify
	Mouth . . . illustrious [17]

❖ 亦	{1496} apple
	Not to be confused with the more complex character with the same meaning (FRAME 1642), the primitive meaning of **apple** will help eliminate the abstract meaning of the key word, *likewise.* [6]

2973 奕	radiating vitality
	Apple . . . St. Bernard dog. [9]

2974	indication

跡 Let this key word connote the sort of **indications** or traces detectives look for in compiling their clues. Its elements: *wooden leg . . . apple.* [13]

2975	phraseology

辭 This one is going to take some work, since it is full of odd combinations. The primitives you have to work with are: *claw . . . chop . . . belt . . . elbow . . . crotch . . . chili pepper.* Our suggestion is that you take advantage of what you did with the left half of *chaos,* the very last character of Book 1 (FRAME 1500). [19]

2976	tortoise

龜 The primitive elements you will recognize scattered around this complete character are *bound up,* a pair of *brooms,* and a *sheaf.* For the rest, we leave you to your own devices. [18]

❖ Unlike the drawing of the character, there are NO known component parts to guide your hand here in drawing the primitive element. Once again, take your time with it and maintain the stroke order strictly. [12]

2977	rope (N.)

繩 *Thread . . . tortoise.* [18]

2978		flies
蠅	Insect . . . tortoise. [18]	

Compounds

Compounds

The 26 characters brought together here are best learned in pairs or "compounds." The full term and its meaning is given before each set of characters.

蝴蝶 butterfly

2979	butterfly (front end)
蝴	Since the Chinese word for **butterfly** requires two characters, we may learn them together by taking the first character as the **front end** and the next as the **back end**. The elements you have to work with to remember the **front end** (the head, thorax, and forewings are): *insect . . . recklessly.* [15]
2980	butterfly (back end)
蝶	And here are the elements for remembering the **butterfly's back end** (the abdomen and hind wings): *insect . . . family tree.* [15]

蜘蛛 spider

2981	spider (front end)
蜘	*Insect . . . know.* Think of a black widow **spider**. The **front end** is the part that *knows* an intruder is in the neighborhood. [14]
2982	spider (back end)
蛛	*Insect . . . vermilion.* The **back end** of the black widow **spider** is the part that has the *vermilion*-colored hourglass shape on its underside. [12]

駱駝 camel

2983 駱 *Horse . . . each.* [16]	camel (front end)
2984 駝 *Horse . . . it.* [15]	camel (back end)

蜻蜓 dragonfly

2985 蜻 *Insect . . . blue or green / telescope.* [14]	dragonfly (front end)
2986 蜓 *Insect . . . royal court.* [13]	dragonfly (back end)

鳳凰 phoenix

2987 鳳 *Wind . . . ceiling . . . bird.* [14]	male phoenix
2988 凰 *Wind . . . emperor.* [11]	female phoenix

橄欖 olive

2989 橄 *Tree . . . brave.* [16]	olive (A)
2990 欖 *Tree . . . magnifying glass.* [25]	olive (B)

玻璃 glass

2991 玻	glass (front side)
	Jewel . . . covering. [9]
2992 璃	glass (back side)
	Jewel . . . Fagin. [14]

咖啡 coffee

2993 咖	coffee (first drop)
	Mouth . . . add. [8]
2994 啡	coffee (last drop)
	Mouth . . . jail cell. [11]

葡萄 grapes

2995 葡	grapes (A)
	Flowers . . . bound up . . . dog tag. [13]
2996 萄	grapes (B)
	Flowers . . . canteen. [12]

吩咐 instruct

2997 吩	in-
	Mouth . . . part. [7]
2998 咐	-struct
	Mouth . . . pay. [8]

丘兵 ping-pong

This combination of characters is used as the informal
name for the game of table tennis.

2999		ping
丘	Left-legged *troop*. [6]	
3000		pong
兵	Right-legged *troop*. [6]	

Postscripts

POSTSCRIPT 1

IF YOU HAVE made your way successfully through all 3,000 characters covered in the foregoing lessons, you have every right to heave a great sigh of relief. But before you get too comfortable, there are a couple of Postscripts we would like to add.

First of all, in compiling a list of characters for these books, the primary criterion was frequency of use. At the same time, other considerations persuaded us to allow a small number of characters to slip in that fell just shy of our frequency criteria. Some of them helped reinforce the learning of important primitive elements. Others helped clarify the special method of ordering followed in these pages. Still others were just so simple to learn that we could not resist making an exception of them.

In the process, another group of characters that by virtue of frequency belonged in the lessons had to be set aside. There are 35 of them in all, and we have gathered them together for you here. Of these, 20 are used as surnames, some of them very common, and another 10 appear in various kinds of proper names.

We recommend that you think of the following pages as a first real-world challenge to the skills you have picked up in the course of these two books. Once you have passed this test, a second Postscript awaits you for a final touch.

We begin with the 20 surnames. In three cases, the romanization of the name is identical to a key word that appears in an earlier lesson but with a different character. These are marked with a "-2".

3001	崔 [11]	Cui
	You will recognize this character as the primitive element meaning *pterodactyl* (page 98).	
3002	曹 [11]	Cao
	As a primitive element, we learned this character with the meaning *cadet* (page 115).	

3003	劉	[15]	Liu
3004	潘	[15]	Pan
3005	梁	[11]	Liang
3006	沈	[7]	Shen
3007	鄭	[15]	Zheng
3008	譚	[19]	Tam
3009	趙	[14]	Zhao
3010	姚	[9]	Yao-2
3011	魯	[15]	Lu
3012	姜	[9]	Jiang-2
3013	范	[9]	Fan
3014	薛	[17]	Xue
3015	涂	[10]	Tu

3016	彭	[12]	Peng
3017	郁	[19]	Yu-2
3018	馮	[12]	Feng
3019	魏	[18]	Wei
3020	岳	[9]	Yue

The characters in the next 10 frames are often met in proper names. They are presented in no particular order.

3021	彿	[8]	as though
3022	莉	[11]	jasmine
	Often used in girls' names.		
3023	湘	[12]	Hunan Province
	An abbreviation for the province's name.		
3024	甸	[17]	outlying areas
3025	滄	[13]	dark blue
3026	穆	[16]	reverent

3027	娜 [10]	*na*
	The character is often used to transliterate the sound *na* as it appears in names such as An*na* and Dia*na*.	

3028	瓊 [19]	fine jade

3029	琳 [14]	gem
	Often used in girls' names.	

3030	鈞 [12]	30 catties
	An ancient unit of weight amounting to roughly 15 kilograms (see FRAME 856). It often appears in boys' names.	

And to conclude, five miscellaneous characters.

3031	喲 [12]	Oh!
	An exclamation indicating mild surprise.	

3032	砲 [10]	cannon

3033	蒐 [14]	search for

芙蓉 cottonrose hibiscus

3034	芙 [8]	hibiscus (A)

3035	蓉 [14]	cottonrose hibiscus (B)

Postscript 2

To end on a suitably serious note, we have included a special character that does not show up among the nearly 50,000 characters covered in the largest modern dictionaries of the Chinese language. The character, which is reduplicated to refer to a type of noodles famous in Shaanxi Province, is said to be the most complex Chinese character around today and has become the stuff of legend. There is even a mnemonic ditty about its drawing order.

And so here it is, a story to end all stories:

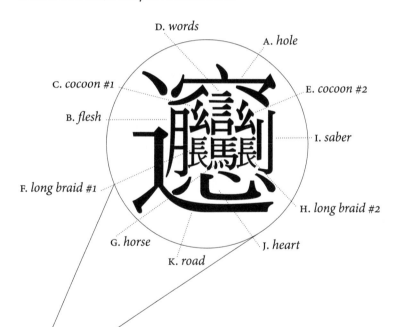

D. *words*

A. *hole*

C. *cocoon #1*

E. *cocoon #2*

B. *flesh*

I. *saber*

F. *long braid #1*

H. *long braid #2*

G. *horse*

J. *heart*

K. *road*

50,001

Biang

Perhaps you have heard of the celebrated Chinese singer and songwriter Flank Chinatra, known throughout the land for such timeless hits as "Hong Kong, Hong Kong," "Strangers in Shanghai" (in the local dialect, "Strangers in the Nai"), and "Mai Wei."

Now the story is told of a strange dream Flank had one night that led to the composition of one of his most famous ballads. Chinatra recalls in his memoirs that he dreamed he was traveling a back *road* that led to the city of Guangzhou astride his magnificent *horse*, **Biang**, who trotted proudly, its tail woven into two *long braids* fluttering in the breeze. Suddenly and without warning his mount collapsed and died. Days passed without anyone appearing on the deserted *road*, and Flank grew weak and disoriented.

On the verge of starvation, and in an act of desperation, he unsheathed his trusty *saber*, cut a *hole* in the *flesh* of the *horse*, and took out the *heart* to eat. Leaning against the carcass, he began to croon a dirge for the poor departed beast. The *words* of the song carried to two *cocoons* nearby, inspiring the beautiful butterflies inside to break out and take flight. Thinking it a good omen, Flank cried out in his sleep: "Fly me to Guangzhou!" He awoke in a cold sweat and immediately put the *words* to paper, forever immortalizing his legendary horse **Biang**.

Don't be surprised if you hear noodle vendors whistling the tune as they slap their **Biang Biang** noodles into shape. [57]

Indexes

Hand-Drawn Characters

This Index presents all the characters in this book in the order of their appearance. They are printed in one of the typical type styles used to teach children how to draw characters with a pen or pencil—the same form used in this book to show proper stroke order. The pronunciation (Mandarin) of the character is given beneath. Some of the characters have multiple pronunciations, which can be found by consulting a dictionary under the pronunciation given here.

叭	咕	咱	串	罩	囂	顛	叨	刮	盯
bā	*gū*	*zán*	*chuàn*	*zhào*	*xiāo*	*diān*	*dāo*	*guā*	*dīng*
1501	1502	1503	1504	1505	1506	1507	1508	1509	1510
呵	姦	嬰	姑	姆	兢	碩	砌	哨	晃
hē	*jiān*	*yīng*	*gū*	*mǔ*	*jīng*	*shuò*	*qì*	*shào*	*huǎng*
1511	1512	1513	1514	1515	1516	1517	1518	1519	1520
泊	汰	沾	渺	腺	坦	娃	涯	吋	肘
bó	*tài*	*zhān*	*miǎo*	*xiàn*	*tǎn*	*wá*	*yá*	*cùn*	*zhǒu*
1521	1522	1523	1524	1525	1526	1527	1528	1529	1530
灼	炒	澆	哩	鯉	嘿	丹	喧	賓	濱
zhuó	*chǎo*	*jiāo*	*lǐ*	*lǐ*	*hēi*	*dān*	*xuān*	*bīn*	*bīn*
1531	1532	1533	1534	1535	1536	1537	1538	1539	1540
寡	棚	柏	槓	朵	杜	桂	椅	杰	櫻
guǎ	*péng*	*bǎi*	*gàng*	*duǒ*	*dù*	*guì*	*yǐ*	*jié*	*yīng*
1541	1542	1543	1544	1545	1546	1547	1548	1549	1550
梢	桐	宋	淋	焚	昧	朱	株	樑	碟
shāo	*tóng*	*Sòng*	*lìn*	*fén*	*mèi*	*zhū*	*zhū*	*liáng*	*dié*
1551	1552	1553	1554	1555	1556	1557	1558	1559	1560
萌	苛	膜	寞	暮	燃	咒	獸	狸	嗅
méng	*kē*	*mó*	*mò*	*mù*	*rán*	*zhòu*	*shòu*	*lí*	*xiù*
1561	1562	1563	1564	1565	1566	1567	1568	1569	1570

牡	牢	贊	舍	啥	洽	旺	碧	汪	柱
mǔ	láo	zàn	shè	shá	qià	wàng	bì	wāng	wǎng
1571	1572	1573	1574	1575	1576	1577	1578	1579	1580
珠	噩	鱷	鬥	栓	柱	鉤	鈔	銷	鎖
zhū	è	è	dòu	shuān	zhù	gōu	chāo	xiāo	suǒ
1581	1582	1583	1584	1585	1586	1587	1588	1589	1590
鑽	迫	逼	逃	逞	轟	軌	軋	輻	煎
zuàn	pò	bī	táo	chěng	hōng	guǐ	yà	fú	jiān
1591	1592	1593	1594	1595	1596	1597	1598	1599	1600
喻	榆	略	暈	渾	膏	亨	哼	淳	鯨
yù	yú	lüè	yūn	hún	gāo	hēng	hēng	chún	jīng
1601	1602	1603	1604	1605	1606	1607	1608	1609	1610
贖	晝	津	鰲	枚	牧	玫	敦	諾	謂
shú	zhòu	jīn	lí	méi	mù	méi	dūn	nuò	wèi
1611	1612	1613	1614	1615	1616	1617	1618	1619	1620
詢	罰	訂	詠	諜	註	諒	讚	貳	膩
xún	fá	dìng	yǒng	dié	zhù	liàng	zàn	èr	nì
1621	1622	1623	1624	1625	1626	1627	1628	1629	1630
洩	划	嘎	域	栽	戚	蔑	喊	濺	址
xiè	huá	gā	yù	zāi	qī	miè	hǎn	jiàn	zhǐ|
1631	1632	1633	1634	1635	1636	1637	1638	1639	1640
澀	蘋	赴	趟	堤	鍵	婿	裁	襪	滾
sè	píng	fù	tàng	dī	jiàn	xù	cái	wà	gǔn
1641	1642	1643	1644	1645	1646	1647	1648	1649	1650
衰	衷	禪	猿	吊	帕	帖	帆	幅	錦
shuāi	zhōng	chán	yuán	diào	pà	tiě	fān	fú	jīn
1651	1652	1653	1654	1655	1656	1657	1658	1659	1660
沛	柿	鬧	棘	棗	蕾	吞	妖	沃	轎
pèi	shì	nào	jí	zǎo	lěi	tūn	yāo	wò	jiào
1661	1662	1663	1664	1665	1666	1667	1668	1669	1670
垃	啼	蒂	滴	頃	匙	乖	乘	剩	棍
lā	tí	dì	dī	qǐng	chí	guāi	chéng	shèng	gùn
1671	1672	1673	1674	1675	1676	1677	1678	1679	1680

諧	柴	敏	霉	迄	砍	坎	炊	欽	剖
xié	chái	mǐn	méi	qì	kǎn	kǎn	chuī	qīn	pōu
1681	1682	1683	1684	1685	1686	1687	1688	1689	1690
菩	芒	荒	謊	茫	贏	訊	坊	芳	訪
pú	máng	huāng	huǎng	máng	yíng	xùn	fáng	fāng	fǎng
1691	1692	1693	1694	1695	1696	1697	1698	1699	1700
熬	菸	榜	磅	膀	銳	虹	蝠	蛙	蝗
áo	yān	bǎng	bàng	bǎng	ruì	hóng	fú	wā	huáng
1701	1702	1703	1704	1705	1706	1707	1708	1709	1710
蟬	楓	胞	炮	袍	雹	逐	遂	蒙	朦
chán	fēng	bāo	pào	páo	báo	zhú	suì	měng	méng
1711	1712	1713	1714	1715	1716	1717	1718	1719	1720
豪	啄	琢	嫁	腸	楊	燙	蕩	詳	羨
háo	zhuó	zhuó	jià	cháng	yáng	tàng	dàng	xiáng	xiàn
1721	1722	1723	1724	1725	1726	1727	1728	1729	1730
唯	堆	焦	瞧	礁	蕉	雕	截	准	雀
wéi	duī	jiāo	qiáo	jiāo	jiāo	diāo	jié	zhǔn	què
1731	1732	1733	1734	1735	1736	1737	1738	1739	1740
霍	奮	奪	翹	塌	翰	咽	姻	廟	廂
huò	fèn	duó	qiào	tā	hàn	yān	yīn	miào	xiāng
1741	1742	1743	1744	1745	1746	1747	1748	1749	1750
嘛	磨	廈	廁	悟	忠	悼	慎	恕	悄
ma	mó	shà	cè	wù	zhōng	dào	shèn	shù	qiǎo
1751	1752	1753	1754	1755	1756	1757	1758	1759	1760
恍	惰	恢	恒	慕	恰	惶	愉	愈	惑
huǎng	duò	huī	héng	mù	qià	huáng	yú	yù	huò
1761	1762	1763	1764	1765	1766	1767	1768	1769	1770
怔	怖	添	悔	慌	悅	憎	忌	惟	懼
zhēng	bù	tiān	huǐ	huāng	yuè	zēng	jì	wéi	jù
1771	1772	1773	1774	1775	1776	1777	1778	1779	1780
患	惹	恩	憶	媳	熄	瑟	泌	蜜	摩
huàn	rě	ēn	yì	xí	xī	sè	mì	mì	mó
1781	1782	1783	1784	1785	1786	1787	1788	1789	1790

蛾	扒	扣	捐	拍	啪	損	扛	扎	拇
é	pá	kòu	juān	pāi	pā	sǔn	káng	zhā	mǔ
1791	1792	1793	1794	1795	1796	1797	1798	1799	1800
拘	抄	拓	捏	撓	抹	描	摸	挑	拴
jū	chāo	tuò	niē	náo	mǒ	miáo	mō	tiǎo	shuān
1801	1802	1803	1804	1805	1806	1807	1808	1809	1810
拾	搭	掠	捨	拭	扯	拖	揚	搞	撞
shí	dā	lüè	shě	shì	chě	tuō	yáng	gǎo	zhuàng
1811	1812	1813	1814	1815	1816	1817	1818	1819	1820
摘	捆	撼	擾	擅	壇	顫	莽	戒	械
zhāi	kǔn	hàn	rǎo	shàn	tán	chàn	mǎng	jiè	xiè
1821	1822	1823	1824	1825	1826	1827	1828	1829	1830
誡	奔	噴	墳	憤	材	孕	扔	圾	叉
jiè	bēn	pēn	fén	fèn	cái	yùn	rēng	jī	chā
1831	1832	1833	1834	1835	1836	1837	1838	1839	1840
桑	嗓	寇	敲	灌	權	毅	肢	妓	歧
sāng	sǎng	kòu	qiāo	guàn	quán	yì	zhī	jì	qí
1841	1842	1843	1844	1845	1846	1847	1848	1849	1850
翅	淑	椒	后	盾	販	扳	覓	妥	睬
chì	shū	jiāo	hòu	dùn	fàn	bān	mì	tuǒ	cǎi
1851	1852	1853	1854	1855	1856	1857	1858	1859	1860
允	勾	晉	宏	胎	冶	颱	怠	抬	丟
yǔn	gōu	jìn	hóng	tāi	yě	tái	dài	tái	diū
1861	1862	1863	1864	1865	1866	1867	1868	1869	1870
臺	致	撤	硫	琉	疏	蔬	崩	岩	崎
tái	zhì	chè	liú	liú	shū	shū	bēng	yán	qí
1871	1872	1873	1874	1875	1876	1877	1878	1879	1880
崖	炭	碳	盼	頒	芬	扮	岔	頌	訟
yá	tàn	tàn	pàn	bān	fēn	bàn	chà	sòng	sòng
1881	1882	1883	1884	1885	1886	1887	1888	1889	1890
翁	裕	榕	賞	嘗	嚐	掌	擋	膛	頗
wēng	yù	róng	shǎng	cháng	cháng	zhǎng	dǎng	táng	pō
1891	1892	1893	1894	1895	1896	1897	1898	1899	1900

坡	披	彼	皺	雛	趨	菠	殖	殊	殘
pō	pī	bǐ	zhòu	chú	qū	bō	zhí	shū	cán
1901	1902	1903	1904	1905	1906	1907	1908	1909	1910
咧	裂	耿	恥	輯	攝	娶	扶	熙	腎
liě	liè	gěng	chǐ	jí	shè	qǔ	fú	xī	shèn
1911	1912	1913	1914	1915	1916	1917	1918	1919	1920
募	脅	劣	勳	勸	劫	怒	茄	彷	征
mù	xié	liè	xūn	quàn	jié	nù	qié	fǎng	zhēng
1921	1922	1923	1924	1925	1926	1927	1928	1929	1930
徒	徊	徵	懲	循	徹	役	衍	衡	銜
tú	huái	zhēng	chéng	xún	chè	yì	yǎn	héng	xián
1931	1932	1933	1934	1935	1936	1937	1938	1939	1940
禿	頹	秒	稍	穌	蘇	萎	黏	黎	漆
tū	tuí	miǎo	shāo	sū	sū	wěi	nián	lí	qī
1941	1942	1943	1944	1945	1946	1947	1948	1949	1950
膝	稠	稿	穎	稅	稼	菌	稚	穫	私
xī	chóu	gǎo	yǐng	shuì	jià	jùn	zhì	huò	sī
1951	1952	1953	1954	1955	1956	1957	1958	1959	1960
秩	殼	穀	鍬	揪	梨	犁	曆	糕	糊
zhì	ké	gǔ	qiāo	jiū	lí	lí	lì	gāo	hú
1961	1962	1963	1964	1965	1966	1967	1968	1969	1970
粘	糧	菊	糙	粒	燦	粉	瞇	幣	斃
zhān	liáng	jú	cāo	lì	càn	fěn	mī	bì	bì
1971	1972	1973	1974	1975	1976	1977	1978	1979	1980
蔽	撇	弊	筍	筒	築	笨	箭	筋	伍
bì	piě	bì	sǔn	tǒng	zhù	bèn	jiàn	jīn	wǔ
1981	1982	1983	1984	1985	1986	1987	1988	1989	1990
仇	倡	伯	仲	估	偵	俱	側	佑	佐
chóu	chàng	bó	zhòng	gū	zhēn	jù	cè	yòu	zuǒ
1991	1992	1993	1994	1995	1996	1997	1998	1999	2000
仔	俏	倘	倚	佳	侍	伙	宿	伏	袱
zǐ	qiào	tǎng	yǐ	jiā	shì	huǒ	sù	fú	fú
2001	2002	2003	2004	2005	2006	2007	2008	2009	2010

偷	伐	佩	佈	僑	億	傾	侮	倍	仿
tōu	*fá*	*pèi*	*bù*	*qiáo*	*yì*	*qīng*	*wǔ*	*bèi*	*fǎng*
2011	2012	2013	2014	2015	2016	2017	2018	2019	2020
傲	僧	悠	俄	儀	侄	仙	俗	償	臥
ào	*sēng*	*yōu*	*é*	*yí*	*zhí*	*xiān*	*sú*	*cháng*	*wò*
2021	2022	2023	2024	2025	2026	2027	2028	2029	2030
傍	俺	淹	掩	催	摧	攜	符	貸	荷
bàng	*ǎn*	*yān*	*yǎn*	*cuī*	*cuī*	*xié*	*fú*	*dài*	*hé*
2031	2032	2033	2034	2035	2036	2037	2038	2039	2040
仗	杖	夾	俠	頰	狹	挾	峽	傘	聚
zhàng	*zhàng*	*jiā*	*xiá*	*jiá*	*xiá*	*xié*	*xiá*	*sǎn*	*jù*
2041	2042	2043	2044	2045	2046	2047	2048	2049	2050
挫	劍	斂	撿	簽	儉	萊	葛	褐	竭
cuò	*jiàn*	*liǎn*	*jiǎn*	*qiān*	*jiǎn*	*lái*	*gé*	*hé*	*jié*
2051	2052	2053	2054	2055	2056	2057	2058	2059	2060
歇	揭	淫	挺	瓦	瓷	瓶	鋁	宮	瑩
xiē	*jiē*	*yín*	*tǐng*	*wǎ*	*cí*	*píng*	*lǚ*	*gōng*	*yíng*
2061	2062	2063	2064	2065	2066	2067	2068	2069	2070
螢	撈	煥	旋	吻	匆	錫	惕	屑	尿
yíng	*lāo*	*huàn*	*xuán*	*wěn*	*cōng*	*xī*	*tì*	*xiè*	*suī*
2071	2072	2073	2074	2075	2076	2077	2078	2079	2080
刷	犀	遲	漏	屁	履	屎	屏	屈	掘
shuā	*xī*	*chí*	*lòu*	*pì*	*lǚ*	*shǐ*	*píng*	*qū*	*jué*
2081	2082	2083	2084	2085	2086	2087	2088	2089	2090
尺	眉	媚	肩	妒	淚	啓	扇	奈	款
chǐ	*méi*	*mèi*	*jiān*	*dù*	*lèi*	*qǐ*	*shàn*	*nài*	*kuǎn*
2091	2092	2093	2094	2095	2096	2097	2098	2099	2100
祟	祝	祥	祕	慰	蔚	蒜	棕	宙	軸
suì	*zhù*	*xiáng*	*mì*	*wèi*	*wèi*	*suàn*	*zōng*	*zhòu*	*zhóu*
2101	2102	2103	2104	2105	2106	2107	2108	2109	2110
袖	笛	坤	呻	暢	夥	巢	棵	裸	裹
xiù	*dí*	*kūn*	*shēn*	*chàng*	*huǒ*	*cháo*	*kē*	*luǒ*	*guǒ*
2111	2112	2113	2114	2115	2116	2117	2118	2119	2120

析	晰	芹	折	哲	逝	誓	欣	掀	祈
xī	*xī*	*qín*	*zhé*	*zhé*	*shì*	*shì*	*xīn*	*xiān*	*qí*
2121	2122	2123	2124	2125	2126	2127	2128	2129	2130
慚	嶄	拆	炸	詐	妻	淒	棲	煞	捷
cán	*zhǎn*	*chāi*	*zhà*	*zhà*	*qī*	*qī*	*qī*	*shà*	*jié*
2131	2132	2133	2134	2135	2136	2137	2138	2139	2140
秉	剝	彙	兼	賺	嫌	謙	歉	廉	鐮
bǐng	*bō*	*huì*	*jiān*	*zhuàn*	*xián*	*qiān*	*qiàn*	*lián*	*lián*
2141	2142	2143	2144	2145	2146	2147	2148	2149	2150
簾	睜	掙	箏	塘	逮	隸	慷	糠	耍
lián	*zhēng*	*zhēng*	*zhēng*	*táng*	*dài*	*lì*	*kāng*	*kāng*	*shuǎ*
2151	2152	2153	2154	2155	2156	2157	2158	2159	2160
耐	喘	揣	糟	遭	槽	抖	庸	傭	甩
nài	*chuǎn*	*chuǎi*	*zāo*	*zāo*	*cáo*	*dǒu*	*yōng*	*yōng*	*shuǎi*
2161	2162	2163	2164	2165	2166	2167	2168	2169	2170
惜	措	棄	燕	遮	畔	拌	叛	券	藤
xī	*cuò*	*qì*	*yàn*	*zhē*	*pàn*	*bàn*	*pàn*	*quàn*	*téng*
2171	2172	2173	2174	2175	2176	2177	2178	2179	2180
狀	牆	鼎	寢	侵	浸	贓	藏	臟	獎
zhuàng	*qiáng*	*dǐng*	*qǐn*	*qīn*	*jìn*	*zāng*	*cáng*	*zàng*	*jiǎng*
2181	2182	2183	2184	2185	2186	2187	2188	2189	2190
漿	槳	蔣	淵	肅	嘯	蕭	鏽	芝	貶
jiāng	*jiǎng*	*jiǎng*	*yuān*	*sù*	*xiào*	*xiāo*	*xiù*	*zhī*	*biǎn*
2191	2192	2193	2194	2195	2196	2197	2198	2199	2200
泛	歪	矯	矮	唉	埃	挨	簇	茅	橘
fàn	*wāi*	*jiǎo*	*ǎi*	*ài*	*āi*	*ái*	*cù*	*máo*	*jú*
2201	2202	2203	2204	2205	2206	2207	2208	2209	2210
舒	弘	夷	姨	疆	僵	薑	粥	沸	拂
shū	*hóng*	*yí*	*yí*	*jiāng*	*jiāng*	*jiāng*	*zhōu*	*fèi*	*fú*
2211	2212	2213	2214	2215	2216	2217	2218	2219	2220
剃	涕	梯	朽	聘	犧	姊	躺	躲	躬
tì	*tì*	*tī*	*xiǔ*	*pìn*	*xī*	*zǐ*	*tǎng*	*duǒ*	*gōng*
2221	2222	2223	2224	2225	2226	2227	2228	2229	2230

嗜	拷	暑	睹	賭	奢	堵	煮	諸	儲
shì	kǎo	shǔ	dǔ	dǔ	shē	dǔ	zhǔ	zhū	chǔ
2231	2232	2233	2234	2235	2236	2237	2238	2239	2240
屠	署	薯	歸	篩	棺	爹	斧	咬	狡
tú	shǔ	shǔ	guī	shāi	guān	diē	fǔ	yǎo	jiǎo
2241	2242	2243	2244	2245	2246	2247	2248	2249	2250
趴	踏	踐	蹄	捉	踩	蹦	跌	促	踢
pā	tà	jiàn	tí	zhuō	cǎi	bèng	diē	cù	tī
2251	2252	2253	2254	2255	2256	2257	2258	2259	2260
躁	噪	澡	藻	操	燥	躍	戳	耀	猾
zào	zào	zǎo	zǎo	cāo	zào	yuè	chuō	yào	huá
2261	2262	2263	2264	2265	2266	2267	2268	2269	2270
髓	髒	渦	鍋	蝸	禍	陌	隙	陡	障
suǐ	zāng	wō	guō	wō	huò	mò	xì	dǒu	zhàng
2271	2272	2273	2274	2275	2276	2277	2278	2279	2280
陪	隧	墜	陋	挖	窯	窺	窟	窄	榨
péi	suì	zhuì	lòu	wā	yáo	kuī	kū	zhǎi	zhà
2281	2282	2283	2284	2285	2286	2287	2288	2289	2290
窘	窮	窩	腔	累	螺	紗	綽	紹	絮
jiǒng	qióng	wō	qiāng	lèi	luó	shā	chuò	shào	xù
2291	2292	2293	2294	2295	2296	2297	2298	2299	2300
繞	紮	綿	繪	絡	綢	絨	締	紫	繁
rào	zā	mián	huì	luò	chóu	róng	dì	zǐ	fán
2301	2302	2303	2304	2305	2306	2307	2308	2309	2310
紡	繭	纏	緻	繫	納	紛	縮	綜	紳
fǎng	jiǎn	chán	zhì	jì	nà	fēn	suō	zōng	shēn
2311	2312	2313	2314	2315	2316	2317	2318	2319	2320
緣	緒	絞	緩	暖	援	索	勃	脖	繳
yuán	xù	jiǎo	huǎn	nuǎn	yuán	suǒ	bó	bó	jiǎo
2321	2322	2323	2324	2325	2326	2327	2328	2329	2330
邀	繡	蘿	鑼	邏	籮	蠻	頸	莖	勁
yāo	xiù	luó	luó	luó	luó	mán	jǐng	jīng	jìng
2331	2332	2333	2334	2335	2336	2337	2338	2339	2340

徑	溪	幼	幽	濕	玄	畜	蓄	牽	弦
jìng	xī	yòu	yōu	shī	xuán	chù	xù	qiān	xián
2341	2342	2343	2344	2345	2346	2347	2348	2349	2350
磁	滋	慈	譏	爍	遜	卸	御	禦	卵
cí	zī	cí	jī	shuò	xùn	xiè	yù	yù	luǎn
2351	2352	2353	2354	2355	2356	2357	2358	2359	2360
孵	乳	浮	俘	卿	貿	榴	疑	礙	凝
fū	rǔ	fú	fú	qīng	mào	liú	yí	ài	níng
2361	2362	2363	2364	2365	2366	2367	2368	2369	2370
擬	玲	鈴	伶	嶺	桶	誦	湧	踴	卷
nǐ	líng	líng	líng	lǐng	tǒng	sòng	yǒng	yǒng	juàn
2371	2372	2373	2374	2375	2376	2377	2378	2379	2380
圈	捲	倦	範	怨	宛	腕	婉	碗	詭
quān	juǎn	juàn	fàn	yuàn	wǎn	wàn	wǎn	wǎn	guǐ
2381	2382	2383	2384	2385	2386	2387	2388	2389	2390
跪	輿	酬	酌	酷	醇	醋	醉	粹	翠
guì	yú	chóu	zhuó	kù	chún	cù	zuì	cuì	cuì
2391	2392	2393	2394	2395	2396	2397	2398	2399	2400
碎	酸	梭	峻	俊	釁	醬	猶	奠	蹲
suì	suān	suō	jùn	jùn	xìn	jiàng	yóu	diàn	dūn
2401	2402	2403	2404	2405	2406	2407	2408	2409	2410
逗	豈	凱	豎	嘉	嘻	盟	孟	猛	盛
dòu	qǐ	kǎi	shù	jiā	xī	méng	mèng	měng	shèng
2411	2412	2413	2414	2415	2416	2417	2418	2419	2420
盞	盒	盜	盪	寧	盈	盆	盃	蘊	濫
zhǎn	hé	dào	dàng	níng	yíng	pén	bēi	yùn	làn
2421	2422	2423	2424	2425	2426	2427	2428	2429	2430
鑑	尷	尬	拋	耽	枕	覽	攬	纜	狠
jiàn	gān	gà	pāo	dān	zhěn	lǎn	lǎn	lǎn	hěn
2431	2432	2433	2434	2435	2436	2437	2438	2439	2440
恨	爵	嚼	懇	墾	豹	貓	貌	朗	狼
hèn	jué	jiáo	kěn	kěn	bào	māo	mào	lǎng	láng
2441	2442	2443	2444	2445	2446	2447	2448	2449	2450

飢 jī 2451	饒 ráo 2452	飾 shì 2453	飲 yǐn 2454	蝕 shí 2455	飽 bǎo 2456	饅 mán 2457	餅 bǐng 2458	餃 jiǎo 2459	餓 è 2460
潛 qián 2461	蠶 cán 2462	溉 gài 2463	慨 kǎi 2464	萍 píng 2465	秤 chèng 2466	淆 yáo 2467	艾 ài 2468	哎 āi 2469	拔 bá 2470
攀 pān 2471	屯 tún 2472	頓 dùn 2473	噸 dūn 2474	純 chún 2475	居 jiè 2476	齒 chǐ 2477	齣 chū 2478	齡 líng 2479	洶 xiōng 2480
籬 lí 2481	辜 gū 2482	宰 zǎi 2483	辨 biàn 2484	辯 biàn 2485	臂 bì 2486	劈 pī 2487	譬 pì 2488	僻 pì 2489	譯 yì 2490
擇 zé 2491	澤 zé 2492	墊 diàn 2493	摯 zhì 2494	糾 jiū 2495	凌 líng 2496	菱 líng 2497	陵 líng 2498	咳 ké 2499	剎 shā 2500
嚷 rǎng 2501	釀 niàng 2502	塞 sài 2503	寨 zhài 2504	憲 xiàn 2505	晴 qíng 2506	猜 cāi 2507	靖 jìng 2508	債 zhài 2509	蹟 jī 2510
牲 shēng 2511	隆 lóng 2512	腥 xīng 2513	猩 xīng 2514	醒 xǐng 2515	瞎 xiā 2516	轄 xiá 2517	契 qì 2518	拜 bài 2519	潔 jié 2520
蜂 fēng 2521	峰 fēng 2522	鋒 fēng 2523	逢 féng 2524	蓬 péng 2525	縫 féng 2526	奏 zòu 2527	湊 còu 2528	秦 qín 2529	蠢 chǔn 2530
捧 pěng 2531	嘆 tàn 2532	艱 jiān 2533	灘 tān 2534	畢 bì 2535	唾 tuò 2536	吟 yín 2537	貪 tān 2538	琴 qín 2539	栗 lì 2540
潭 tán 2541	遷 qiān 2542	覆 fù 2543	飄 piāo 2544	闆 bǎn 2545	闊 kuò 2546	閉 bì 2547	潤 rùn 2548	閣 gé 2549	擱 gē 2550
闡 chǎn 2551	閱 yuè 2552	悶 mēn 2553	閃 shǎn 2554	閥 fá 2555	閘 zhá 2556	闢 pì 2557	蒼 cāng 2558	搶 qiǎng 2559	菲 fěi 2560

輩	悲	徘	殲	籤	纖	喉	猴	韓	違
bèi	bēi	pái	jiān	qiān	xiān	hóu	hóu	hán	wéi
2561	2562	2563	2564	2565	2566	2567	2568	2569	2570
緯	竿	罕	軒	肝	刊	汗	桿	悍	徐
wěi	gān	hǎn	xuān	gān	kān	hàn	gǎn	hàn	xú
2571	2572	2573	2574	2575	2576	2577	2578	2579	2580
敘	塗	斜	喇	嗽	賴	懶	嫩	煉	鍊
xù	tú	xié	lǎ	sòu	lài	lǎn	nèn	liàn	liàn
2581	2582	2583	2584	2585	2586	2587	2588	2589	2590
腫	董	鍾	痰	症	疼	癒	疫	癌	疲
zhǒng	dǒng	zhōng	tán	zhèng	téng	yù	yì	ái	pí
2591	2592	2593	2594	2595	2596	2597	2598	2599	2600
疾	痴	瘤	痕	癢	癱	瘡	穩	隱	癮
jí	chī	liú	hén	yǎng	tān	chuāng	wěn	yǐn	yǐn
2601	2602	2603	2604	2605	2606	2607	2608	2609	2610
巨	渠	拒	矩	距	框	筐	砸	匯	匠
jù	qú	jù	jǔ	jù	kuàng	kuāng	zá	huì	jiàng
2611	2612	2613	2614	2615	2616	2617	2618	2619	2620
匪	匿	兜	嘔	毆	軀	昂	抑	葵	僚
fěi	nì	dōu	ǒu	ōu	qū	áng	yì	kuí	liáo
2621	2622	2623	2624	2625	2626	2627	2628	2629	2630
遼	瞭	療	瞪	凳	澄	潑	撥	杉	彬
liáo	liào	liáo	dèng	dèng	chéng	pō	bō	shān	bīn
2631	2632	2633	2634	2635	2636	2637	2638	2639	2640
衫	彰	膨	趁	診	滲	膠	謬	寥	斑
shān	zhāng	péng	chèn	zhěn	shèn	jiāo	miù	liáo	bān
2641	2642	2643	2644	2645	2646	2647	2648	2649	2650
紋	鏟	薩	脊	函	涵	映	殃	肥	爬
wén	chǎn	sà	jǐ	hán	hán	yìng	yāng	féi	pá
2651	2652	2653	2654	2655	2656	2657	2658	2659	2660
疤	艷	甜	鉗	媒	煤	謀	棋	欺	旗
bā	yàn	tián	qián	méi	méi	móu	qí	qī	qí
2661	2662	2663	2664	2665	2666	2667	2668	2669	2670

嘶	撕	堪	勘	遣	譴	囊	潰	櫃	宜
sī	sī	kān	kān	qiǎn	qiǎn	náng	kuì	guì	yí
2671	2672	2673	2674	2675	2676	2677	2678	2679	2680

誼	租	粗	阻	疊	壘	鋤	叢	樸	撲
yì	zū	cū	zǔ	dié	lěi	chú	cóng	pǔ	pū
2681	2682	2683	2684	2685	2686	2687	2688	2689	2690

僕	譜	哄	洪	烘	恭	拱	暴	瀑	爆
pú	pǔ	hǒng	hóng	hōng	gōng	gǒng	bào	pù	bào
2691	2692	2693	2694	2695	2696	2697	2698	2699	2700

殿	戴	翼	糞	撰	啞	壺	蟹	懈	購
diàn	dài	yì	fèn	zhuàn	yǎ	hú	xiè	xiè	gòu
2701	2702	2703	2704	2705	2706	2707	2708	2709	2710

溝	鑰	籲	冊	刪	柵	珊	遍	偏	淪
gōu	yào	yù	cè	shān	zhà	shān	biàn	piān	lún
2711	2712	2713	2714	2715	2716	2717	2718	2719	2720

倫	抵	呡	哺	鋪	輔	捕	敷	浦	蒲
lún	dǐ	máng	bǔ	pù	fǔ	bǔ	fū	pǔ	pú
2721	2722	2723	2724	2725	2726	2727	2728	2729	2730

薄	簿	傅	縛	郭	廓	鄙	耶	爺	郊
bó	bù	fù	fù	guō	kuò	bǐ	yē	yé	jiāo
2731	2732	2733	2734	2735	2736	2737	2738	2739	2740

邦	綁	郵	鄧	擲	廊	擁	緞	刁	叼
bāng	bǎng	yóu	dèng	zhì	láng	yōng	duàn	diāo	diāo
2741	2742	2743	2744	2745	2746	2747	2748	2749	2750

殷	壽	濤	鑄	禱	籌	伺	飼	舶	航
yīn	shòu	tāo	zhù	dǎo	chóu	cì	sì	bó	háng
2751	2752	2753	2754	2755	2756	2757	2758	2759	2760

艇	艦	艙	沿	鉛	狐	辦	溢	暇	霞
tǐng	jiàn	cāng	yán	qiān	hú	bàn	yì	xiá	xiá
2761	2762	2763	2764	2765	2766	2767	2768	2769	2770

氧	氛	氯	氫	鞏	霸	壩	勒	鞠	靴
yǎng	fēn	lù	qīng	gǒng	bà	bà	lē4	jū	xuē
2771	2772	2773	2774	2775	2776	2777	2778	2779	2780

鞭	芽	訝	撐	雅	邪	奧	澳	懊	悉
biān	yá	yà	chēng	yǎ	xié	ào	ào	ào	xī
2781	2782	2783	2784	2785	2786	2787	2788	2789	2790
竊	審	嬸	毯	毫	耗	耕	籍	藉	托
qiè	shěn	shěn	tǎn	háo	hào	gēng	jí	jiè	tuō
2791	2792	2793	2794	2795	2796	2797	2798	2799	2800
畏	喂	脹	帳	肆	鬍	鬆	鵬	鳴	鴻
wèi	wèi	zhàng	zhàng	sì	hú	sōng	péng	míng	hóng
2801	2802	2803	2804	2805	2806	2807	2808	2809	2810
鴿	鶴	鶯	鵲	鷗	鴉	鵝	烏	嗚	搗
gē	hè	yīng	què	ōu	yā	é	wū	wū	dǎo
2811	2812	2813	2814	2815	2816	2817	2818	2819	2820
寓	愚	偶	屬	勵	鋼	崗	綱	逆	溯
yù	yú	ǒu	lì	lì	gāng	gǎng	gāng	nì	sù
2821	2822	2823	2824	2825	2826	2827	2828	2829	2830
塑	缸	罐	鬱	鹽	鹹	掏	淘	陶	謠
sù	gāng	guàn	yù	yán	xián	tāo	táo	táo	yáo
2831	2832	2833	2834	2835	2836	2837	2838	2839	2840
冤	饞	挽	勉	橡	豫	騰	碼	馴	瑪
yuān	chán	wǎn	miǎn	xiàng	yù	téng	mǎ	xún	mǎ
2841	2842	2843	2844	2845	2846	2847	2848	2849	2850
駐	驕	馳	螞	憑	駛	騷	駕	騾	駁
zhù	jiāo	chí	mǎ	píng	shǐ	sāo	jià	luó	bó
2851	2852	2853	2854	2855	2856	2857	2858	2859	2860
闖	驅	騙	驟	遞	虜	虐	膚	盧	爐
chuǎng	qū	piàn	zhòu	dì	lǔ	nüè	fū	lú	lú
2861	2862	2863	2864	2865	2866	2867	2868	2869	2870
蘆	驢	虧	污	愕	誇	垮	跨	獻	融
lú	lú	kuī	wū	è	kuā	kuǎ	kuà	xiàn	róng
2871	2872	2873	2874	2875	2876	2877	2878	2879	2880
隔	濾	慶	薦	傑	瞬	麟	憐	鄰	曬
gé	lǜ	qìng	jiàn	jié	shùn	lín	lián	lín	shài
2881	2882	2883	2884	2885	2886	2887	2888	2889	2890

灑	罷	擺	唇	辱	震	振	魄	槐	魅
sǎ	bà	bǎi	chún	rǔ	zhèn	zhèn	pò	huái	mèi
2891	2892	2893	2894	2895	2896	2897	2898	2899	2900
瑰	魂	愧	魁	醜	壟	寵	龐	攏	聾
guī	hún	kuì	kuí	chǒu	lǒng	chǒng	páng	lǒng	lóng
2901	2902	2903	2904	2905	2906	2907	2908	2909	2910
籠	插	毀	舅	椿	鑿	鼠	竄	臘	蠟
lóng	chā	huǐ	jiù	zhuāng	záo	shǔ	cuàn	là	là
2911	2912	2913	2914	2915	2916	2917	2918	2919	2920
獵	艘	嫂	瘦	搜	稻	蹈	滔	陷	焰
liè	sōu	sǎo	shòu	sōu	dào	dǎo	tāo	xiàn	yàn
2921	2922	2923	2924	2925	2926	2927	2928	2929	2930
餡	輛	瞞	爽	綴	碰	挪	誣	譽	嶼
xiàn	liàng	mán	shuǎng	zhuì	pèng	nuó	wū	yù	yǔ
2931	2932	2933	2934	2935	2936	2937	2938	2939	2940
傻	磚	惠	穗	曠	礦	擴	聰	蔥	膽
shǎ	zhuān	huì	suì	kuàng	kuàng	kuò	cōng	cōng	dǎn
2941	2942	2943	2944	2945	2946	2947	2948	2949	2950
瞻	摟	屢	濁	燭	觸	囑	欄	攔	蹤
zhān	lǒu	lǚ	zhuó	zhú	chù	zhǔ	lán	lán	zōng
2951	2952	2953	2954	2955	2956	2957	2958	2959	2960
聳	劑	齋	擠	鈕	羞	紐	脾	啤	碑
sǒng	jì	zhāi	jǐ	niǔ	xiū	niǔ	pí	pí	bēi
2961	2962	2963	2964	2965	2966	2967	2968	2969	2970
赫	嚇	奕	跡	辭	龜	繩	蠅	蝴	蝶
hè	xià	yì	jì	cí	guī	shéng	yíng	hú	dié
2971	2972	2973	2974	2975	2976	2977	2978	2979	2980
蜘	蛛	駱	駝	蜻	蜓	鳳	凰	橄	欖
zhī	zhū	luò	tuó	qīng	tíng	fèng	huáng	gǎn	lǎn
2981	2982	2983	2984	2985	2986	2987	2988	2989	2990
玻	璃	咖	啡	葡	萄	吩	咐	乒	乓
bō	lí	kā	fēi	pú	táo	fēn	fù	pīng	pāng
2991	2992	2993	2994	2995	2996	2997	2998	2999	3000

崔	曹	劉	潘	梁	沈	鄭	譚	趙	姚
cuī	*cáo*	*liú*	*pān*	*liáng*	*shěn*	*zhèng*	*tán*	*zhào*	*yáo*
3001	3001	3003	3004	3005	3006	3007	3008	3009	3010
魯	姜	范	薛	涂	彭	郁	馮	魏	岳
lǔ	*jiāng*	*fàn*	*xuē*	*tú*	*péng*	*yù*	*féng*	*wèi*	*yuè*
3011	3012	3013	3014	3015	3016	3017	3018	3019	3020
佛	莉	湘	甸	滄	穆	娜	瓊	琳	鈞
fú	*lì*	*xiāng*	*diàn*	*cāng*	*mù*	*nà*	*qióng*	*lín*	*jūn*
3021	3022	3023	3024	3025	3026	3027	3028	3029	3030
哟	砲	蒐	芙	蓉	邊				
yō	*pào*	*sōu*	*fú*	*róng*	*biāng*				
3031	3032	3033	3034	3035	50,001				

INDEX II

Primitive Elements

This Index lists all the primitive elements used in Books 1 and 2. Characters used as primitives are only listed if the writing is significantly altered. The primitives are arranged according to the number of strokes. The number refers to the page on which the element is first introduced.

1 劃

′			㇄	㇄	⼃	㇇
1.31	1.32	1.57	1.57	1.248	1.349

33

2 劃 *cf 29*

八	儿	几	勹	˅	ナ	刂	刂	厂
1.39	1.39	1.40	1.40	1.40	1.50	1.52	1.52	1.65

冂	人	宀	亠	口	⺀	冫	⺈	乂
1.88	1.114	1.134	1.136	1.166	1.168	1.168	1.176	1.214

厂	厶	亻	㇀	丂	与	卩	卩	マ
1.217	1.219	1.240	1.248	1.276	1.278	1.292	1.293	1.293

巴	メ	凵	丩	ユ	匚
1.294	1.303	1.303	1.306	1.323	1.329

3 劃 *cf 31*

亠	屮	少	巛	川	氵	宀	犭	亼
1.49	1.62	1.63	1.69	1.69	1.70	1.90	1.108	1.115

辶	夂	弋	乏	巴	口	广	忄	扌
1.128	1.131	1.147	1.158	1.194	1.202	1.203	1.204	1.209

卅	艹	犬	云	彳	尸	彐	厶	阝
1.211	1.211	1.212	1.220	1.233	1.253	1.263	1.263	1.282

幺	丰	彡	⻖	乡	毛	凡	尢	亏
1.289	1.314	1.332	1.348	1.348	1.356	2.50	2.153	2.216

4劃
cf 34

毌	巛	朩	艹	生	亢	攴	㐄	㐅
1.60	1.80	1.94	1.99	1.111	1.136	1.142	1.154	1.161
氏	小	开	殳	灬	云	从	壬	牛
1.161	1.204	1.211	1.216	1.218	1.221	1.246	1.248	1.250
衤	尹	丱	爿	屮	罓	臼	旡	丶
1.256	1.264	1.268	1.271	1.278	1.285	1.295	1.301	1.311
丰	夬	卬	八	氐	月	亠	尢 (3)	气
1.313	1.323	1.330	1.334	1.357	1.372	2.138	2.153	2.201

5劃
cf 23

氺	氺	言	戊	疋	疋	礻	帀	弗
1.70	1.70	1.137	1.149	1.157	1.159	1.161	1.165	1.275
宀	刃	卯	皿	艮	先	朮	丼	夫
1.284	1.292	1.292	1.298	1.299	1.307	1.308	1.309	1.314
广	癶	参	虫	冊	氏	肀	台	冂
1.329	1.330	1.332	1.337	1.345	1.346	1.349	1.350	1.357
丄	卉	夗						
1.358	2.70	2.146						

6劃
cf 29

圭	叩	刖	吉	聿	聿	戋	戌	亦
1.78	1.109	1.130	1.139	1.141	1.141	1.149	1.150	1.161
束	虫	羊	羊	严	行	并	扩	关
1.166	1.193	1.196	1.197	1.219	1.233	1.249	1.252	1.270
自	糸	艮	良	冊	产	出	缶	虍
1.279	1.286	1.299	1.300	1.316	1.333	1.361	1.362	1.365

关 1.368	白 1.370	业 1.371	囟 1.373	未 2.204	夸 2.216	舛 2.218

7劃 *cf 20*

亠 1.137	豖 1.195	㐬 1.221	庀 1.269	𧾷 1.280	坙 1.289	甬 1.294	𦥑 1.295	酉 1.296
無 1.337	釆 1.355	镸 1.358	庐 1.366	囟 1.375	曼 2.117	矣 2.121	孛 2.138	孚 2.143
夋 2.149	豕 2.155	夆 2.166						

8劃 *cf 9*

車 1.37	泉 1.71	戔 1.152	帛 1.164	霝 1.167	音 1.181	佳 1.198	尚 1.226	臤 1.231
彖 1.263	食 1.301	业 1.340	侖 1.344	㸚 1.371	延 1.377	豖 2.55	奄 2.95	隶 2.112
卒 2.148	変 2.162	匋 2.211	臽 2.224	乖 2.48	虎 1.365			

9劃 *cf 11* 若

畐 1.54	枼 1.101	俞 1.130	复 1.178	易 1.196	崔 1.199	曷 1.247	奂 1.251	耑 1.266
咼 1.281	壴 1.297	亲 1.305	柬 1.327	段 1.351	禺 1.361	爰 2.137	兹 2.141	叟 2.223

10劃 *cf 8*

烛 1.249	离 1.304	寅 1.310	冓 1.343	專 1.347	隹 1.360	䂂 1.362	芻 2.79	鬲 2.217
臽 2.224	高 2.33	旁 2.53						

11劃 *cf 6*

商 1.172	執 1.307	董 1.315	菫 1.315	殷 1.353	絲 1.371	妻 1.376	奎 2.59	泰 2.85

	敝	崔	尉	曹	鹵	鹿		
	2.88	2.96	2.105	2.113	2.210	*1.366*		

| 12劃 | 戠 | 惠 | 黍 | 奈 | 業 | 舞 | 黽 | | |
| *cf 4* | 1.182 | 1.234 | 2.84 | 2.180 | 2.189 | 2.218 | 2.231 | *電 13 ? Radical 205* | |

| 13劃 | 僉 | 與 | 辟 | 蜀 | 宣 | 貢 | 壘 | 梟 | 敦 |
| *cf 4* | 1.246 | 1.303 | 1.305 | 1.376 | 2.69 | 2.70 | 2.122 | 2.128 | 2.139 |

	睪	肅
	2.161	*2.121*

| 14劃 | 蒦 | 臧 | 翟 | 悤 | |
| *cf 2* | 1.215 | 2.117 | 2.129 | 2.177 | *1.378* |

| 15劃 | 晶 | 鼠 |
| *cf 2* | 2.187 | 2.223 |

| 17劃 | 闌 | 鐵 | 龠 |
| *cf 1(2)* | 1.376 | 2.171 | 2.192 |

| 18劃 | 蓳 |
| *none* | 1.216 |

| 19劃 | 戀 | *先集* |
| *none* | 1.288 | *2.25* |

INDEX III

Characters by Number of Strokes

Here you will find all the characters treated in Books 1 and 2, grouped by the number of strokes. The ordering within each stroke-number group follows the standard dictionary practice of arranging the characters according to "radicals."

1 劃

一 1
乙 91

2 劃

丁 86
七 7
乃 582
九 9
了 95
二 2
人 736
入 638
八 8
刀 79
刁 2749
力 687
匕 419
十 10
卜 42
又 589

3 劃

丈 776
三 3
上 44
下 45
丸 41

久 778
之 921
乞 434
也 476
于 1230
亡 457
凡 59
刃 80
勺 65
千 37
叉 1840
及 584
口 11
土 147
士 307
夕 108
大 106
女 96
子 92
寸 153
小 103
山 634
川 123
工 72
己 485
已 488
巾 382
干 1225
弓 941
才 578

4 劃

不 924
丑 1489
中 36
丹 1537
乏 922
予 936
云 395
互 629
五 5
井 1312
什 743
仁 761
仇 1991
今 1186
介 241
仍 751
允 1861
元 56
內 639
公 643
六 6
冗 288
凶 1113
分 641
切 81
勾 62
勻 1862
化 815
勿 771
匹 1250

升 39
午 509
友 590
反 607
天 403
太 120
夫 679
夭 404
孔 93
少 104
尤 226
尹 882
尺 2091
屯 2472
巨 2611
巴 1279
幻 1347
引 903
心 942
戈 529
戶 335
手 830
扎 548
支 1799
文 601
斗 1270
斤 893
方 856
日 461
曰 12
日 1499
月 13

木 191
欠 439
止 353
歹 661
比 422
毛 1381
氏 1328
水 126
火 157
爪 612
父 968
片 914
牙 1374
牛 235
犬 225
王 248
瓦 2065

5 劃

且 1297
世 27
丘 1003
丙 780
主 259
乍 865
乎 1106
仔 2001
他 752
仗 2041
付 766

仙	2027	巧	950	乓	3000	在	581	米 724
代	769	市	388	交	969	地	478	羊 495
令	1050	布	383	亥	1136	圾	1839	羽 511
以	796	平	1103	亦	1496	多	109	老 954
兄	101	幼	2343	仰	1255	夷	2213	考 955
冊	2714	弘	2212	仲	1994	她	477	而 887
冬	402	必	547	件	750	好	97	耳 666
凸	31	扒	1792	任	793	如	98	肉 782
凹	30	打	559	份	738	妄	459	肌 60
出	635	扔	1838	仿	2020	字	180	臣 683
刊	2576	斥	863	伊	883	存	580	自 32
功	692	且	29	伍	1990	宅	1383	至 626
加	695	未	202	伏	2009	宇	1231	舌 38
包	489	末	203	伐	2012	守	181	舟 1350
匆	2076	本	200	休	753	安	186	色 1283
北	420	正	362	伙	2007	寺	155	艾 2468
半	907	母	99	全	257	尖	107	血 1075
占	43	民	1334	合	245	州	124	行 699
卡	46	永	127	企	358	巡	272	衣 375
印	1059	汁	138	充	630	帆	1658	西 1191
去	624	犯	1056	兆	223	年	806	迄 1685
古	16	玄	2346	兇	1114	式	333	迅 270
句	63	玉	249	先	239	忙	544	
另	688	瓜	1355	光	119	成	341	**7 劃**
叨	1508	甘	1285	共	1306	托	2800	
只	50	生	1163	再	1318	扛	1798	串 1504
叫	1130	用	896	冰	401	扣	1793	亨 1607
召	82	甩	2170	刑	576	收	1131	伯 1993
叭	1501	田	14	划	1632	旨	429	估 1995
叮	87	由	845	列	662	早	25	伴 908
可	88	甲	848	劣	1923	旬	64	伶 2374
台	621	申	850	匠	2620	旭	26	伸 851
史	586	白	33	危	1057	曲	892	伺 2757
右	74	皮	656	灰	158	有	75	似 797
司	1348	目	15	吃	435	朱	1557	但 747
叼	2750	矛	931	各	281	朵	1545	佈 2014
囚	737	矢	927	吉	308	朽	2224	位 749
四	4	石	114	吊	1655	次	443	低 1332
外	111	示	834	时	1529	此	426	住 748
央	1277	禾	710	同	176	死	664	佐 2000
失	682	穴	995	名	112	每	431	佑 1999
奴	693	立	408	后	1854	汗	2577	佔 739
奶	583			吐	151	江	137	何 1232
孕	1837	**6 劃**		向	178	池	479	余 946
它	428			吸	585	污	2874	佛 868
尼	821	丢	1870	回	520	百	34	作 868
左	73	乒	2999	因	518	竹	728	你 741

姆	1515	披	1902	武	360	肢	1848	俠	2044
始	623	抬	1869	歧	1850	肥	2659	信	754
姐	1298	抱	555	氓	2723	肩	2094	冒	175
姑	1514	抵	2722	氛	2772	肯	357	冠	293
姓	1165	抹	1806	沛	1661	育	631	剃	2221
委	719	押	849	沫	204	臥	2030	則	84
孟	2418	抽	846	河	144	舍	1574	削	118
季	718	拂	2220	沸	2219	芙	3034	前	277
孤	1356	拆	2133	油	847	芬	1886	剎	2500
宗	840	拇	1800	治	622	花	772	勁	2340
官	966	拉	570	沼	135	芳	1699	勃	2328
宙	2109	抛	2434	沾	1523	芹	2123	勇	1055
定	364	拌	2177	沿	2764	芽	2782	勉	2844
宛	2386	拍	1795	況	143	虎	1422	南	1200
宜	2680	拐	690	泊	1521	表	1161	卸	2357
尚	179	拓	1803	泌	1788	衫	2641	卻	1042
居	826	拔	2470	法	625	軋	1598	厚	113
屆	2476	拖	1817	泡	490	迫	1592	叛	2178
屈	2089	拘	1801	波	657	述	1141	咧	1911
岡	1403	招	558	泣	409	采	614	咬	2249
岩	1879	放	463	泥	823	金	261	咱	1503
岳	3020	斧	2248	注	260	長	1387	咳	2499
岸	1226	於	465	泳	133	門	1201	咸	346
帕	1656	旺	1577	炊	1688	阻	2684	咽	1747
帖	1657	昂	2627	炎	160	阿	981	哀	377
幸	1127	昆	423	炒	1532	附	989	品	21
底	1333	昇	40	爬	2660	雨	396	哄	2693
店	523	昌	23	爭	876	青	1151	哇	152
府	767	明	20	爸	1281	非	1212	哈	246
延	371	昏	1330	版	915			哎	2469
弦	2350	易	818	牧	1616			型	577
彼	1903	昔	897	物	817	**9 劃**		垮	2877
彿	3021	朋	19	狀	2181			城	342
往	704	服	1044	狐	2766	亭	299	奏	2527
征	1930	杯	926	狗	232	亮	300	契	2518
忠	1756	杰	1549	玩	252	侮	2018	奕	2973
念	1188	東	473	玫	1617	侯	1216	姚	3010
忽	816	松	644	的	66	侵	2185	姜	3012
怔	1771	板	608	盲	458	侶	801	姦	1512
怕	543	枉	1580	直	68	便	775	姨	2214
怖	1772	析	2121	知	929	係	1040	姻	1748
性	1166	枕	2436	祈	2130	促	2259	姿	445
怪	1494	林	192	秉	2141	俄	2024	威	344
或	336	枚	1615	空	998	俊	2405	娃	1527
房	831	果	853	糾	2495	俏	2002	孩	1138
所	857	枝	603	者	959	俗	2028	客	283
承	1372	欣	2128	股	600	俘	2364	宣	184
						保	764		

室	627	既	1101	珍	1266	胞	1713	首	67
封	154	星	1164	甚	1291	胡	17	香	717
屋	824	映	2657	界	242	苗	221		
屍	820	春	1171	畏	2801	苛	1562	**10 劃**	
屎	2087	昧	1556	疤	2661	若	212		
屏	2088	昨	867	疫	2598	苦	214	乘	1678
差	501	昭	83	皆	425	英	1278	修	1269
巷	1309	是	368	皇	254	茂	340	俯	768
帝	413	枯	197	盃	2428	范	3013	俱	1997
帥	963	架	697	盆	2427	茄	1928	俺	2032
幽	2344	柄	781	盈	2426	茅	2209	倆	1451
度	905	柏	1543	相	199	虐	2867	倉	1209
建	370	某	1286	盼	1884	虹	1707	個	757
彥	1272	染	209	盾	1855	衍	1938	倍	2019
待	703	柔	932	省	121	要	1192	們	1202
很	1085	查	207	眉	2092	訂	1623	倒	760
徊	1932	柱	1586	看	549	計	322	倘	2003
律	700	柳	1049	眨	923	貞	53	候	1217
後	1029	柵	2716	矩	2614	負	61	倚	2004
怎	866	柿	1662	砂	115	赴	1643	借	898
怒	1927	歪	2202	砌	1518	趴	2251	倡	1992
思	535	殃	2658	砍	1686	軌	1597	倦	2383
怠	1868	段	1345	研	573	軍	290	倫	2721
急	870	毒	1149	祕	2104	迷	725	值	745
怨	2385	泉	129	祖	1300	追	962	兼	2144
恒	1764	洋	497	祝	2102	退	1089	冤	2841
恍	1761	洗	240	神	852	送	1440	准	1739
恢	1763	洛	286	秋	714	逃	1594	凌	2496
恨	2441	洞	177	科	895	逆	2829	凍	475
恰	1766	津	1613	秒	1943	迴	521	剖	1690
扁	1322	洩	1631	穿	1375	郁	3017	剛	1404
拜	2519	洪	2694	突	997	郊	2740	剝	2142
括	562	洲	134	竿	2572	郎	1342	匪	2621
拭	1815	洶	2480	紀	1015	酉	1063	卿	2365
拱	2697	活	141	約	1017	重	1242	原	130
拴	1810	洽	1576	紅	1016	陋	2283	員	54
拷	2232	派	610	級	1014	陌	2277	哥	89
拼	799	炭	1882	缸	2832	降	993	哨	1519
拾	1811	炮	1714	美	496	限	1091	哩	1534
持	561	炸	2134	耍	2160	面	1363	哪	1459
指	560	為	1385	耐	2161	革	1365	哭	229
按	568	牲	2511	耶	2738	韋	1221	哲	2125
挑	1809	狠	2440	肺	389	音	449	哺	2724
挖	2285	狡	2250	胃	28	頁	57	哼	1608
政	363	玲	2372	背	421	風	483	唇	2894
故	316	玻	2991	胎	1865	飛	1362	唉	2205
施	812	珊	2717	胖	909	食	1096	唐	879

埃	2206	挪	2937	海	433	紐	2967	躬	2230
埋	171	挫	2051	浸	2186	純	2475	軒	2574
夏	285	振	2897	涂	3015	紗	2297	辱	2895
套	1390	挺	2064	消	142	紙	1329	透	721
娘	1095	挽	2843	涉	355	紛	2317	逐	1717
娛	1370	挾	2047	涕	2222	素	1150	途	1235
娜	3027	捆	1822	烈	663	紡	2311	逗	2411
孫	1041	捉	2255	烏	2818	索	2327	這	332
宮	2069	捏	1804	烘	2695	缺	1405	通	1054
宰	2483	捐	1794	烤	956	翁	1891	逛	273
害	1167	捕	2727	爹	2247	翅	1851	逝	2126
宴	187	效	970	特	236	耕	2797	逞	1595
宵	185	料	894	狸	1569	耗	2796	速	1237
家	492	旁	466	狹	2046	耽	2435	造	271
容	649	旅	811	狼	2450	耿	1913	逢	2524
射	952	時	156	珠	1581	胸	1115	連	275
屑	2079	晃	1520	班	940	能	1432	酌	2394
展	1392	晉	1863	瓶	2067	脂	430	配	1062
峰	2522	書	311	瓷	2066	脅	1922	酒	1061
島	1399	朗	2449	畔	2176	脆	1058	釘	265
峻	2404	柴	1682	留	1046	脈	611	針	264
峽	2048	栓	1585	畜	2347	脊	2654	閃	2554
師	964	栗	2540	畝	779	臭	231	關	1457
席	904	校	972	畢	2535	致	1872	陡	2279
帶	390	株	1558	疲	2600	航	2760	院	990
座	786	核	1137	疼	2596	般	1352	陣	991
庫	524	根	1086	疾	2601	茫	1695	除	1234
庭	795	格	282	病	1247	茶	243	隻	592
弱	944	栽	1635	症	2595	草	213	飢	2451
徐	2580	桂	1547	益	1357	荒	1693	馬	1415
徑	2341	桃	224	真	71	蚊	1271	骨	978
徒	1931	框	2616	眠	1335	衰	1651	高	296
恐	539	案	201	砲	3032	衷	1652	鬥	1584
恕	1759	桌	211	破	659	袁	378	鬼	1441
恥	1914	桐	1552	砸	2618	袍	1715		
恩	1783	桑	1841	崇	2101	袖	2111	**11 劃**	
恭	2696	殊	1909	祥	2103	被	660	乾	436
息	538	殷	2751	租	2682	訊	1697	假	1358
悄	1760	氣	1360	秤	2466	討	324	偉	1223
悅	1776	氧	2771	秦	2529	訓	325	偏	2719
悍	2579	泰	1172	秩	1961	託	1384	做	746
悔	1774	流	632	窄	2289	記	487	停	759
悟	1755	浦	2729	站	410	豈	2412	健	758
扇	2098	浩	238	笑	729	豹	2446	側	1998
拳	912	浪	1094	粉	1977	財	579	偵	1996
拿	550	浮	2363	紋	2651	貢	77	偶	2823
挨	2207	浴	646	納	2316	起	491		

誌	534	鼻	575	慶	2883	潰	2678	處	1424
認	532	齊	1487	憂	542	澄	2636	蝗	1710
誓	2127			憎	1777	澆	1533	蝠	1708
誘	722	**15 劃**		憐	2888	熟	298	蝦	1359
語	328			憤	1835	熬	1701	蝴	2979
誠	1831	僵	2216	戲	1425	熱	1134	蝶	2980
誣	2938	價	1198	摩	1790	獎	2190	蝸	2275
誤	1371	僻	2489	摯	2494	瑩	2070	衛	1224
誦	2377	儀	2025	撈	2072	瘡	2607	衝	1246
說	469	億	2016	撐	2784	瘤	2603	褲	525
豪	1721	儉	2056	撒	901	皺	1904	誕	372
貌	2448	劇	1426	撓	1805	瞎	2516	誰	505
賓	1539	劈	2487	撕	2672	碼	2848	課	854
赫	2971	劉	3003	撞	1820	磅	1704	誼	2681
趕	1229	劍	2052	撤	1873	稻	2926	調	330
趙	3009	屬	2824	撥	2638	稼	1956	談	331
輔	2726	嘲	49	撫	1296	稿	1953	請	1153
輕	1028	嘶	2671	播	1380	穀	1963	諒	1627
辣	1238	嘻	2416	撰	2705	窮	2292	論	1325
適	417	嘿	1536	撲	2690	窯	2286	諸	2239
遭	2165	噴	1833	敵	418	箭	1988	豎	2414
遮	2175	墜	2284	敷	2728	箱	730	豬	961
遷	2542	增	471	數	1479	範	2384	賜	819
鄙	2737	墨	174	暫	860	篇	1323	賞	1894
酷	2395	墳	1834	暮	1565	糊	1970	賠	447
酸	2402	嬌	407	暴	2698	線	1006	賢	685
銀	1083	審	2792	槳	2192	緞	2748	賣	310
銅	262	寫	1448	槽	2166	締	2308	賤	352
銘	266	寬	215	椿	2915	緣	2321	賦	361
衝	1940	導	269	樂	1035	編	1324	質	862
閣	2549	層	828	樑	1559	緩	2324	賭	2235
閥	2555	履	2086	樓	1480	緯	2571	趟	1644
隙	2278	幟	453	標	1196	罵	1417	趣	668
際	983	廚	1073	樞	1252	罷	2892	踏	2252
障	2280	廟	1749	模	218	膚	2868	踐	2253
需	888	廠	526	樣	500	腔	1899	踢	2260
顧	1900	廢	1261	歐	1253	膜	1563	踩	2256
領	1053	廣	1473	毅	1847	膝	1951	躺	2228
颱	1867	彈	945	毆	2625	膠	2647	輛	2932
餅	2458	影	1263	漿	2191	艘	2922	輝	291
餃	2459	徵	1933	潑	2637	盤	1353	輩	2561
駁	2860	德	707	潔	2520	蔑	1637	輪	1326
魁	2904	徹	1936	潘	3004	蔚	2106	遵	1065
魂	2902	慕	1765	潛	2461	蔣	2193	選	1311
鳳	2987	慧	1169	潤	2548	蔥	2949	遺	1293
鳴	2809	慮	1423	潭	2541	蔭	1190	遼	2631
麼	1038	慰	2105	潮	139	蔽	1981	遲	2083

鄧	2744	噪	2262	燙	1727	輯	1915	艦	2432
鄭	3007	噸	2474	獨	1481	輸	279	嶺	2375
鄰	2889	墾	2445	盧	2869	輻	1599	幫	387
醇	2396	壁	1121	瞞	2933	辦	1119	彌	1454
醉	2398	壇	1826	磚	2942	辨	2484	懇	2444
醋	2397	奮	1742	磨	1752	避	1122	應	1395
鋁	2068	學	1110	禪	1653	還	678	戴	2702
鋒	2523	嶼	2940	穆	3026	邁	1402	擊	636
鋤	2687	憑	2855	穌	1945	邀	2331	擠	2964
鋪	2725	憲	2505	積	1160	醒	2515	擦	844
銳	1706	憶	1784	穎	1954	鋸	827	擬	2371
銷	1589	憾	541	窺	2287	鋼	2826	擱	2550
閱	2552	懂	1243	築	1986	錄	874	斂	2053
隧	2282	懈	2709	篩	2245	錘	1184	斃	1980
隨	985	懊	2789	糕	1969	錢	350	檔	652
震	2896	戰	349	糖	880	錦	1660	檢	787
霉	1684	撼	1823	糙	1974	錯	899	澀	1641
靠	1215	撿	2054	練	1240	錶	1162	濕	2345
鞋	1366	擁	2747	緻	2314	險	984	濟	1488
鞏	2775	擅	1825	縛	2734	雕	1737	濤	2753
養	1100	擇	2491	縫	2526	霍	1741	濫	2430
餓	2460	擋	1898	翰	1746	靈	1461	濱	1540
餘	1233	操	2265	膨	2643	靜	1157	營	804
駐	2851	擔	1478	膩	1630	頭	1067	燥	2266
駕	2858	據	1427	興	1060	頰	2045	燦	1976
駛	2856	整	1239	艙	2763	頸	2338	燭	2955
駝	2984	曆	1968	蔬	1877	頹	1942	爵	2442
髮	1391	曉	168	蕉	1736	頻	356	牆	2182
鬧	1663	樸	2689	蕩	1728	餐	1098	獲	594
魄	2898	樹	1074	融	2880	餡	2931	環	677
魅	2900	橄	2989	螞	2854	館	1099	療	2633
魯	3011	橋	406	螢	2071	駱	2983	癌	2599
鴉	2816	橘	2210	衡	1939	鴨	1398	盪	2424
黎	1949	機	1031	親	1125	默	227	瞧	1734
齒	2477	橡	2845	謀	1625	點	173	瞪	2634
		橫	1474	諧	1681	龍	1444	瞬	2886
		歷	723	諮	446			瞭	2632
16 劃		澡	2263	諷	484			矯	2203
		澤	2492	諾	1619	**17 劃**		礁	1735
儒	889	澳	2788	謀	2667			禦	2359
儘	1077	激	464	謂	1620	償	2029	禮	1069
凝	2370	濁	2954	謎	726	優	762	穗	2944
劑	2962	濃	1439	豫	2846	儲	2240	簇	2208
勳	1924	燃	1566	貓	2447	勵	2825	糞	2704
噓	2196	燈	1258	賴	2586	嚇	2972	糟	2164
嘴	1317	燒	167	蹓	2379	嚐	1896	糠	2159
器	230	燕	2174	蹄	2254	壓	234	縮	2318
噩	1582					嬰	1513		

譴	2676	續	1009	權	1846	變	1026	蠻	2337
贏	1696	纏	2313	邏	2335	顯	1034	觀	595
躁	2261	臟	2189	鑑	2431	驗	1419	釁	2406
辯	2485	蘭	1484	灘	2534	驚	1421	鑰	2712
釋	1377	蠟	2920	癮	2608	髒	2272	饞	2842
鐘	415	蠹	2530	囊	2677	體	1070		
闡	2551	襯	1126	疊	2685	麟	2887		
飄	2544	覽	2437	鑄	2754			**26 劃**	
饒	2452	護	593	竊	2791			讚	1628
馨	1367	臢	2187	鷗	2815	**24 劃**		驢	2872
騷	2857	躍	2267	驕	2852				
鬱	2834	轟	1596	髓	2271	囑	2957		
鹹	2836	辯	1120	灑	2891	壩	2777	**27 劃**	
麵	1364	鏽	2198	聾	2910	攬	2438		
黨	653	鐵	339	籠	2911	癱	2606	纜	2439
齡	2479	闢	2557	讀	329	蘿	2481	鑼	2334
齣	2478	露	977	歡	596	罐	2833	鑽	1591
		霸	2776	聽	708	艷	2662	鍾	1583
		響	1344	彎	1023	蠶	2462		
21 劃		顧	833	攤	1180	讓	1145	**28 劃**	
		驟	2859	襲	1445	釀	2502		
囂	1506	驅	2862			驟	2864	鑿	2916
屬	1482	魔	1442			鷹	1397		
懼	1780	鶯	2813	**23 劃**		鹽	2835		
攜	2037	鶴	2812					**32 劃**	
攝	1916			戀	1025				
櫻	1550			攪	1112	**25 劃**		籲	2713
欄	2958	**22 劃**		曬	2890				
殲	2564			籤	2565	廳	709		
灌	1845	贖	1611	纖	2566	欖	2990	**57 劃**	
爛	1483	顫	1827	蘿	2333	灣	1024	𪚥	50,001
						籮	2336		

INDEX IV
Character Pronunciations

This Index alphabetically lists the pronunciations, with their respective frame numbers, of all the characters treated in Books 1 and 2. Some of the characters have multiple pronunciations, which can be found by consulting a dictionary under the pronunciation given here.

A

ā	阿	981
ā	啊	982
āi	哀	377
āi	埃	2206
āi	哎	2469
ái	挨	2207
ái	癌	2599
ǎi	矮	2204
ài	愛	619
ài	唉	2205
ài	礙	2369
ài	艾	2468
ān	安	186
ǎn	俺	2032
àn	案	201
àn	暗	450
àn	按	568
àn	岸	1226
áng	昂	2627
āo	凹	30
áo	熬	1701
ào	傲	2021
ào	奧	2787
ào	澳	2788
ào	懊	2789

B

bā	八	8
bā	巴	1279
bā	吧	1282
bā	叭	1501
bā	疤	2661
bá	拔	2470
bǎ	把	1280
bà	爸	1281
bà	霸	2776
bà	壩	2777
bà	罷	2892
bái	白	33
bǎi	百	34
bǎi	柏	1543
bǎi	擺	2893
bài	敗	315
bài	拜	2519
bān	班	940
bān	般	1352
bān	搬	1354
bān	扳	1857
bān	頒	1885
bān	斑	2650
bǎn	板	608
bǎn	版	915
bǎn	闆	2545
bàn	半	907
bàn	伴	908
bàn	辦	1119
bàn	扮	1887
bàn	拌	2177
bàn	瓣	2767
bāng	幫	387
bāng	邦	2741
bǎng	榜	1703
bǎng	膀	1705
bǎng	綁	2742
bàng	棒	1174
bàng	磅	1704
bàng	傍	2031
bāo	包	489
bāo	胞	1713
báo	雹	1716
bǎo	保	764
bǎo	堡	765
bǎo	寶	1406
bǎo	飽	2456
bào	抱	555
bào	報	1129
bào	豹	2446
bào	暴	2698
bào	爆	2700
bēi	杯	926
bēi	卑	1491
bēi	盃	2428
bēi	悲	2562
bēi	碑	2970
běi	北	420
bèi	貝	51
bèi	背	421
bèi	被	660
bèi	備	902
bèi	倍	2019
bèi	輩	2561
bēn	奔	1832
běn	本	200
bèn	笨	1987
bēng	崩	1878
bèng	蹦	2257
bī	逼	1593
bí	鼻	575
bǐ	匕	419
bǐ	比	422
bǐ	筆	731
bǐ	彼	1903
bǐ	鄙	2737
bì	必	547
bì	壁	1121
bì	避	1122
bì	碧	1578
bì	幣	1979
bì	斃	1980
bì	蔽	1981
bì	弊	1983
bì	臂	2486
bì	畢	2535
bì	閉	2547
biān	邊	1000
biān	編	1324
biān	鞭	2781
biǎn	扁	1322
biǎn	貶	2200
biàn	便	775
biàn	變	1026
biàn	辯	1120

biàn	辨	2484			chán	禪	1653	chéng	誠	343

dù	杜	1546	fǎ	法	625	fèn	憤	1835	fù	複	437
dù	妒	2095	fǎ	髮	1391	fèn	糞	2704	fù	腹	438
duān	端	891	fān	番	1378	fēng	封	154	fù	復	701
duǎn	短	1068	fān	翻	1379	fēng	風	483	fù	付	766
duàn	斷	1032	fān	帆	1658	fēng	豐	1170	fù	婦	872
duàn	段	1345	fán	凡	59	fēng	瘋	1249	fù	父	968
duàn	鍛	1346	fán	煩	159	fēng	楓	1712	fù	附	989
duàn	緞	2748	fán	繁	2310	fēng	蜂	2521	fù	赴	1643
duī	堆	1732	fǎn	反	607	fēng	峰	2522	fù	覆	2543
duì	兌	467	fǎn	返	609	fēng	鋒	2523	fù	傅	2733
duì	隊	992	fàn	犯	1056	féng	逢	2524	fù	縛	2734
duì	對	1305	fàn	飯	1097	féng	縫	2526	fù	咐	2998
dūn	敦	1618	fàn	販	1856	féng	馮	3018			
dūn	蹲	2410	fàn	泛	2201	fěng	諷	484		**G**	
dūn	頓	2474	fàn	範	2384	fèng	奉	1173	gā	嘎	1633
dùn	盾	1855	fàn	范	3013	fèng	鳳	2987	gà	尬	2433
dùn	頓	2473	fāng	方	461	fó	佛	946	gāi	該	1140
duō	多	109	fāng	芳	1699	fǒu	否	925	gǎi	改	486
duǒ	朵	1545	fáng	妨	462	fū	夫	679	gài	蓋	1078
duǒ	躲	2229	fáng	房	831	fū	孵	2361	gài	概	1102
duó	奪	1743	fáng	防	988	fū	敷	2728	gài	溉	2463
duò	惰	1762	fáng	坊	1698	fū	膚	2868	gān	乾	436
			fǎng	訪	1700	fú	福	837	gān	干	1225
	E		fǎng	彷	1929	fú	服	1044	gān	甘	1285
é	額	284	fǎng	仿	2020	fú	輻	1599	gān	尷	2432
é	蛾	1791	fǎng	紡	2311	fú	幅	1659	gān	竿	2572
é	俄	2024	fàng	放	463	fú	蝠	1708	gān	肝	2575
é	鵝	2817	fēi	非	1212	fú	扶	1918	gǎn	感	540
è	惡	1314	fēi	飛	1362	fú	伏	2009	gǎn	敢	672
è	噩	1582	fēi	啡	2994	fú	袱	2010	gǎn	趕	1229
è	鱷	1583	féi	肥	2659	fú	符	2038	gǎn	桿	2578
è	餓	2460	fěi	菲	2560	fú	拂	2220	gǎn	橄	2989
è	愕	2875	fěi	匪	2621	fú	浮	2363	gàn	幹	1227
ēn	恩	1783	fèi	肺	389	fú	俘	2364	gāng	岡	1403
ér	而	887	fèi	費	947	fú	彿	3021	gāng	剛	1404
ér	兒	1446	fèi	廢	1261	fú	芙	3034	gāng	鋼	2826
ěr	耳	666	fèi	沸	2219	fǔ	府	767	gāng	綱	2828
ěr	爾	1453	fēn	分	641	fǔ	俯	768	gāng	缸	2832
èr	二	2	fēn	芬	1886	fǔ	腐	783	gǎng	港	1310
èr	貳	1629	fēn	紛	2317	fǔ	撫	1296	gǎng	崗	2827
			fēn	氛	2772	fǔ	甫	1336	gàng	槓	1544
	F		fēn	吩	2997	fǔ	斧	2248	gāo	高	296
fā	發	1260	fén	焚	1555	fǔ	輔	2726	gāo	膏	1606
fá	乏	922	fén	墳	1834	fù	負	61	gāo	糕	1969
fá	罰	1622	fěn	粉	1977	fù	副	85	gǎo	搞	1819
fá	伐	2012	fèn	份	738	fù	富	189	gǎo	稿	1953
fá	閥	2555	fèn	奮	1742	fù	賦	361	gào	告	237

gē	哥	89
gē	戈	335
gē	歌	441
gē	割	1168
gē	擱	2550
gē	鴿	2811
gé	格	282
gé	革	1365
gé	葛	2058
gé	閣	2549
gé	隔	2881
gè	各	281
gè	個	757
gěi	給	1011
gēn	跟	1084
gēn	根	1086
gēng	耕	2797
gěng	耿	1913
gèng	更	587
gōng	工	72
gōng	攻	314
gōng	公	643
gōng	功	692
gōng	弓	941
gōng	供	1307
gōng	宮	2069
gōng	躬	2230
gōng	恭	2696
gǒng	拱	2697
gǒng	鞏	2775
gòng	貢	77
gòng	共	1306
gōu	鉤	1587
gōu	勾	1862
gōu	溝	2711
gǒu	狗	232
gòu	夠	110
gòu	構	1321
gòu	購	2710
gū	孤	1356
gū	咕	1502
gū	姑	1514
gū	估	1995
gū	辜	2482
gǔ	古	16
gǔ	股	600

gǔ	谷	645
gǔ	骨	978
gǔ	鼓	1071
gǔ	賈	1197
gǔ	穀	1963
gù	故	316
gù	固	515
gù	雇	832
gù	顧	833
guā	瓜	1355
guā	刮	1509
guǎ	寡	1541
guà	掛	567
guāi	乖	1677
guǎi	拐	690
guài	怪	1494
guān	冠	293
guān	觀	595
guān	官	966
guān	關	1457
guān	棺	2246
guǎn	管	967
guǎn	館	1099
guàn	貫	100
guàn	慣	545
guàn	灌	1845
guàn	罐	2833
guāng	光	119
guǎng	廣	1473
guàng	逛	273
guī	規	680
guī	歸	2244
guī	瑰	2901
guī	龜	2976
guǐ	鬼	1441
guǐ	軌	1597
guǐ	詭	2390
guì	貴	1292
guì	桂	1547
guì	跪	2391
guì	櫃	2679
gǔn	滾	1650
gùn	棍	1680
guō	鍋	2274
guō	郭	2735
guó	國	516

guǒ	果	853
guǒ	裹	2120
guò	過	980

H

hā	哈	246
hái	孩	1138
hǎi	海	433
hài	亥	1136
hài	害	1167
hán	寒	1147
hán	含	1187
hán	韓	2569
hán	函	2655
hán	涵	2656
hǎn	喊	1638
hǎn	罕	2573
hàn	憾	541
hàn	漢	1178
hàn	旱	1228
hàn	翰	1746
hàn	撼	1823
hàn	汗	2577
hàn	悍	2579
háng	行	699
háng	航	2760
háo	豪	1721
háo	毫	2795
hǎo	好	97
hào	浩	238
hào	號	1493
hào	耗	2796
hē	喝	791
hē	呵	1511
hé	和	712
hé	河	144
hé	合	245
hé	禾	710
hé	何	774
hé	核	1137
hé	荷	2040
hé	褐	2059
hé	盒	2422
hè	賀	696
hè	鶴	2812
hè	赫	2971
hēi	黑	172

hēi	嘿	1536
hén	痕	2604
hěn	很	1085
hěn	狠	2440
hèn	恨	2441
hēng	亨	1607
hēng	哼	1608
héng	橫	1474
héng	恒	1764
héng	衡	1939
hōng	轟	1596
hōng	烘	2695
hóng	紅	1016
hóng	虹	1707
hóng	宏	1864
hóng	弘	2212
hóng	洪	2694
hóng	鴻	2810
hǒng	哄	2693
hóu	侯	1216
hóu	喉	2567
hóu	猴	2568
hǒu	吼	94
hòu	厚	113
hòu	後	1029
hòu	候	1217
hòu	后	1854
hū	忽	816
hū	乎	1106
hū	呼	1107
hú	胡	17
hú	湖	145
hú	糊	1970
hú	壺	2707
hú	狐	2766
hú	鬍	2806
hú	蝴	2979
hǔ	虎	1422
hù	護	593
hù	互	629
hù	戶	830
huā	花	772
huá	劃	313
huá	滑	979
huá	華	1181
huá	嘩	1182
huá	划	1632

huá	猾	2270	hùn	混	424	jì	祭	842	jiàn	漸	861
huà	畫	312	huó	活	141	jì	際	983	jiàn	間	1205
huà	話	326	huǒ	火	157	jì	紀	1015	jiàn	濺	1639
huà	化	771	huǒ	伙	2007	jì	繼	1033	jiàn	鍵	1646
huái	懷	546	huǒ	夥	2116	jì	既	1101	jiàn	箭	1988
huái	徊	1932	huò	或	336	jì	濟	1488	jiàn	劍	2052
huái	槐	2899	huò	獲	594	jì	忌	1778	jiàn	踐	2253
huài	壞	380	huò	貨	773	jì	妓	1849	jiàn	鑑	2431
huān	歡	596	huò	霍	1741	jì	繫	2315	jiàn	艦	2762
huán	環	677	huò	惑	1770	jì	劑	2962	jiàn	薦	2884
huán	還	678	huò	穫	1959	jì	跡	2974	jiāng	江	137
huǎn	緩	2324	huò	禍	2276	jiā	家	492	jiāng	漿	2191
huàn	患	1781				jiā	加	695	jiāng	疆	2215
huàn	煥	2073		**J**		jiā	傢	740	jiāng	僵	2216
huàn	喚	809				jiā	佳	2005	jiāng	薑	2217
huàn	換	810	jī	肌	60	jiā	夾	2043	jiāng	姜	3012
huàn	幻	1347	jī	激	464	jiā	嘉	2415	jiǎng	講	1320
huāng	荒	1693	jī	擊	636	jiá	頰	2045	jiǎng	獎	2190
huāng	慌	1775	jī	機	1031	jiǎ	甲	848	jiǎng	槳	2192
huáng	皇	254	jī	雞	1037	jià	架	697	jiǎng	蔣	2193
huáng	煌	255	jī	績	1159	jià	價	1198	jiàng	降	993
huáng	黃	1472	jī	積	1160	jià	假	1358	jiàng	醬	2407
huáng	蝗	1710	jī	基	1289	jià	嫁	1724	jiàng	匠	2620
huáng	惶	1767	jī	圾	1839	jià	稼	1956	jiāo	嬌	407
huǎng	謊	1694	jī	譏	2354	jià	駕	2858	jiāo	教	958
huǎng	恍	1761	jī	飢	2451	jiān	尖	107	jiāo	交	969
huáng	凰	2988	jī	蹟	2510	jiān	堅	686	jiāo	澆	1533
huàng	晃	1520	jí	吉	308	jiān	監	1080	jiāo	焦	1733
huī	灰	158	jí	集	502	jiān	姦	1512	jiāo	礁	1735
huī	輝	291	jí	及	584	jiān	煎	1600	jiāo	蕉	1736
huī	揮	564	jí	急	870	jiān	肩	2094	jiāo	椒	1853
huī	恢	1763	jí	級	1014	jiān	兼	2144	jiāo	膠	2647
huí	迴	521	jí	即	1087	jiān	艱	2533	jiāo	郊	2740
huí	回	520	jí	極	1497	jiān	殲	2564	jiāo	驕	2852
huǐ	悔	1774	jí	棘	1664	jiǎn	剪	278	jiáo	嚼	2443
huǐ	毀	2913	jí	輯	1915	jiǎn	減	347	jiǎo	腳	1043
huì	彙	2143	jí	疾	2601	jiǎn	檢	787	jiǎo	攪	1112
huì	繪	2304	jí	籍	2798	jiǎn	簡	1206	jiǎo	角	1315
huì	匯	2619	jǐ	己	485	jiǎn	揀	1241	jiǎo	矯	2203
huì	惠	2943	jǐ	幾	1030	jiǎn	撿	2054	jiǎo	狡	2250
huì	慧	1169	jǐ	脊	2654	jiǎn	儉	2056	jiǎo	絞	2323
huì	賄	76	jǐ	擠	2964	jiǎn	繭	2312	jiǎo	繳	2330
huì	會	244	jì	寄	188	jiàn	見	55	jiǎo	餃	2459
hūn	昏	1330	jì	計	322	jiàn	賤	352	jiào	較	971
hūn	婚	1331	jì	記	487	jiàn	建	370	jiào	叫	1130
hún	渾	1605	jì	技	602	jiàn	件	750	jiào	轎	1670
hún	魂	2902	jì	寂	606	jiàn	健	758			
			jì	季	718						

kuò	闊	2546	lí	釐	1614	liàng	輛	2932	lóng	聾	2910
kuò	廓	2736	lí	黎	1949	liàng	亮	300	lóng	籠	2911
kuò	擴	2947	lí	梨	1966	liàng	量	170	lǒng	壟	2906
			lí	犁	1967	liáo	聊	1048	lǒng	攏	2909
	L		lí	籬	2481	liáo	僚	2630	lóu	樓	1480
lā	拉	570	lí	璃	2992	liáo	遼	2631	lǒu	摟	2952
lā	啦	571	lǐ	里	169	liáo	療	2633	lòu	漏	2084
lā	垃	1671	lǐ	李	210	liáo	寥	2649	lòu	陋	2283
lǎ	喇	2584	lǐ	理	258	liào	料	894	lú	盧	2869
là	辣	1238	lǐ	裡	376	liào	瞭	2632	lú	爐	2870
là	臘	2919	lǐ	禮	1069	liě	咧	1911	lú	蘆	2871
là	蠟	2920	lǐ	哩	1534	liè	列	662	lǔ	虜	2866
lái	來	789	lǐ	鯉	1535	liè	烈	663	lǔ	魯	3011
lái	萊	2057	lì	立	408	liè	裂	1912	lù	錄	874
lài	賴	2586	lì	力	687	liè	劣	1923	lù	碌	875
lán	籃	1081	lì	利	716	liè	獵	2921	lù	路	976
lán	藍	1082	lì	歷	723	lín	林	192	lù	露	977
lán	蘭	1484	lì	例	756	lín	臨	684	lù	陸	1132
lán	欄	2958	lì	麗	1430	lín	麟	2887	lù	鹿	1428
lán	攔	2959	lì	曆	1968	lín	鄰	2889	lú	驢	2872
lǎn	覽	2437	lì	粒	1975	lín	琳	3029	lǜ	律	700
lǎn	攬	2438	lì	隸	2157	lìn	淋	1554	lǜ	綠	1022
lǎn	纜	2439	lì	栗	2540	líng	零	1052	lǜ	率	1275
lǎn	懶	2587	lì	厲	2824	líng	靈	1461	lǜ	慮	1423
lǎn	欖	2990	lì	勵	2825	líng	玲	2372	lǜ	濾	2882
làn	爛	1483	lì	莉	3022	líng	鈴	2373	lǚ	呂	800
làn	濫	2430	liǎ	倆	1451	líng	伶	2374	lǚ	侶	801
láng	郎	1342	lián	連	275	líng	齡	2479	lǚ	旅	811
láng	狼	2450	lián	蓮	276	líng	凌	2496	lǚ	鋁	2068
láng	廊	2746	lián	聯	1456	líng	菱	2497	lǚ	履	2086
lǎng	朗	2449	lián	廉	2149	líng	陵	2498	lǚ	氯	2773
làng	浪	1094	lián	鐮	2150	lǐng	領	1053	lǚ	屢	2953
lāo	撈	2072	lián	簾	2151	lǐng	嶺	2375	luǎn	卵	2360
láo	勞	803	lián	憐	2888	lìng	另	688	luàn	亂	1500
láo	牢	1572	liǎn	臉	788	lìng	令	1050	lüè	略	1603
lǎo	老	954	liǎn	斂	2053	liū	溜	1047	lüè	掠	1813
le	了	95	liàn	戀	1025	liú	流	632	lún	輪	1326
lēi	勒	2778	liàn	練	1240	liú	留	1046	lún	淪	2720
léi	雷	398	liàn	煉	2589	liú	硫	1874	lún	倫	2721
lěi	蕾	1666	liàn	鍊	2590	liú	琉	1875	lùn	論	1325
lěi	壘	2686	liáng	涼	302	liú	榴	2367	luó	羅	1008
lèi	類	727	liáng	良	1093	liú	瘤	2603	luó	螺	2296
lèi	淚	2096	liáng	樑	1559	liú	劉	3003	luó	蘿	2333
lèi	累	2295	liáng	糧	1972	liǔ	柳	1049	luó	鑼	2334
lěng	冷	1051	liáng	梁	3005	liù	六	6	luó	邏	2335
lí	離	1116	liǎng	兩	1450	lóng	龍	1444	luó	籮	2336
lí	狸	1569	liàng	諒	1627	lóng	隆	2512	luó	騾	2859

luǒ	裸	2119	méi	枚	1615	miè	蔑	1637	nà	娜	3027
luò	洛	286	méi	玫	1617	mín	民	1334	nǎi	乃	582
luò	落	287	méi	霉	1684	mǐn	敏	1683	nǎi	奶	583
luò	絡	2305	méi	眉	2092	míng	明	20	nài	奈	2099
luò	駱	2983	méi	媒	2665	míng	名	112	nài	耐	2161
			méi	煤	2666	míng	銘	266	nán	男	691
M			měi	每	431	míng	鳴	2809	nán	難	1179
mā	媽	1416	měi	美	496	mìng	命	1045	nán	南	1200
má	麻	528	mèi	妹	206	miù	謬	2648	náng	囊	2677
mǎ	馬	1415	mèi	昧	1556	mō	摸	1808	náo	撓	1805
mǎ	碼	2848	mèi	媚	2093	mó	模	218	nǎo	腦	1466
mǎ	瑪	2850	mèi	魅	2900	mó	魔	1442	nǎo	惱	1467
mǎ	螞	2854	mēn	悶	2553	mó	膜	1563	nào	鬧	1663
mà	罵	1417	mén	門	1201	mó	磨	1752	ne	呢	822
ma	嗎	1418	men	們	1202	mó	摩	1790	nèi	內	639
ma	嘛	1751	méng	萌	1561	mǒ	抹	1806	nèn	嫩	2588
mái	埋	171	méng	朦	1720	mò	墨	174	néng	能	1432
mǎi	買	309	méng	盟	2417	mò	末	203	ní	尼	821
mài	賣	310	měng	蒙	1719	mò	沫	204	ní	泥	823
mài	脈	611	měng	猛	2419	mò	莫	217	nǐ	你	741
mài	麥	790	mèng	夢	294	mò	漠	219	nǐ	擬	2371
mài	邁	1402	mèng	孟	2418	mò	默	227	nì	膩	1630
mán	蠻	2337	mī	眯	1978	mò	寞	1564	nì	匿	2622
mán	饅	2457	mí	迷	725	mò	陌	2277	nì	逆	2829
mán	瞞	2933	mí	謎	726	móu	謀	2667	nián	年	806
mǎn	滿	1452	mí	彌	1454	mǒu	某	1286	nián	黏	1948
màn	曼	674	mǐ	米	724	mǔ	母	99	niàn	廿	903
màn	慢	675	mì	密	637	mǔ	畝	779	niàn	念	1188
màn	漫	676	mì	泌	1788	mǔ	姆	1515	niáng	娘	1095
máng	盲	458	mì	蜜	1789	mǔ	牡	1571	niàng	釀	2502
máng	忙	544	mì	覓	1858	mǔ	拇	1800	niǎo	鳥	1396
máng	芒	1692	mì	祕	2104	mù	目	15	niē	捏	1804
máng	茫	1695	mián	棉	386	mù	木	191	nín	您	742
máng	氓	2723	mián	眠	1335	mù	墓	220	níng	凝	2370
mǎng	莽	1828	mián	綿	2303	mù	幕	385	níng	寧	2425
māo	貓	2447	miǎn	免	1411	mù	暮	1565	niú	牛	235
máo	矛	931	miǎn	勉	2844	mù	牧	1616	niǔ	扭	1490
máo	毛	1381	miàn	面	1363	mù	慕	1765	niǔ	鈕	2965
máo	茅	2209	miàn	麵	1364	mù	募	1921	niǔ	紐	2967
mào	冒	175	miáo	苗	221	mù	穆	3026	nóng	農	1438
mào	茂	340	miáo	瞄	222				nóng	濃	1439
mào	帽	384	miáo	描	1807	**N**			nòng	弄	574
mào	貿	2366	miǎo	渺	1524				nú	奴	693
mào	貌	2448	miǎo	秒	1943	ná	拿	550	nǔ	努	694
me	麼	1038	miào	妙	116	nǎ	哪	1459	nǚ	女	96
méi	梅	432	miào	廟	1749	nà	吶	640	nù	怒	1927
méi	沒	598	miè	滅	345	nà	那	1458	nuǎn	暖	2325
						nà	納	2316			

shǐ	使	777	shǔ	署	2242	sòng	宋	1553	tái	台	621

shǐ	使	777	shǔ	署	2242	sòng	宋	1553	tái	台	621
shǐ	矢	927	shǔ	薯	2243	sòng	頌	1889	tái	颱	1867
shǐ	屎	2087	shǔ	鼠	2917	sòng	訟	1890	tái	抬	1869
shǐ	駛	2856	shú	熟	298	sòng	誦	2377	tái	臺	1871
shì	世	27	shú	贖	1611	sōu	艘	2922	tài	太	120
shì	士	307	shù	樹	1074	sōu	搜	2925	tài	泰	1172
shì	式	333	shù	述	1141	sōu	蒐	3033	tài	態	1433
shì	試	334	shù	術	1142	sòu	嗽	2585	tài	汰	1522
shì	是	368	shù	束	1236	sū	穌	1945	tān	攤	1180
shì	市	388	shù	數	1479	sū	蘇	1946	tān	灘	2534
shì	適	417	shù	恕	1759	sú	俗	2028	tān	貪	2538
shì	識	452	shù	豎	2414	sù	宿	2008	tān	癱	2606
shì	室	627	shuā	刷	2081	sù	肅	2195	tán	談	331
shì	示	834	shuǎ	耍	2160	sù	溯	2830	tán	壇	1826
shì	視	836	shuāi	摔	1276	sù	塑	2831	tán	潭	2541
shì	事	878	shuāi	衰	1651	sù	訴	864	tán	痰	2594
shì	勢	1133	shuǎi	甩	2170	sù	素	1150	tán	譚	3008
shì	氏	1328	shuài	帥	963	sù	速	1237	tǎn	坦	1526
shì	釋	1377	shuān	栓	1585	suān	酸	2402	tǎn	毯	2794
shì	柿	1662	shuān	拴	1810	suàn	算	733	tàn	探	1002
shì	拭	1815	shuāng	霜	400	suàn	蒜	2107	tàn	炭	1882
shì	侍	2006	shuāng	雙	591	suī	雖	507	tàn	碳	1883
shì	逝	2126	shuǎng	爽	2934	suī	尿	2080	tàn	嘆	2532
shì	誓	2127	shuǐ	水	126	suí	隨	985	tāng	湯	494
shì	嗜	2231	shuì	睡	1185	suǐ	髓	2271	táng	堂	655
shì	飾	2453	shuì	稅	1955	suì	歲	359	táng	唐	879
shōu	收	1131	shùn	順	125	suì	遂	1718	táng	糖	880
shǒu	首	67	shùn	瞬	2886	suì	崇	2101	táng	膛	1899
shǒu	守	181	shuō	說	469	suì	隧	2282	táng	塘	2155
shǒu	手	548	shuò	碩	1517	suì	碎	2401	tǎng	倘	2003
shòu	售	506	shuò	爍	2355	suì	穗	2944	tǎng	躺	2031
shòu	受	617	sī	思	535	sūn	孫	1041	tàng	趟	1644
shòu	授	618	sī	絲	1005	sǔn	損	1797	tàng	燙	1727
shòu	獸	1568	sī	斯	1290	sǔn	筍	1984	tāo	濤	2753
shòu	壽	2752	sī	司	1348	suō	縮	2318	tāo	掏	2837
shòu	瘦	2924	sī	私	1960	suō	梭	2403	tāo	滔	2928
shū	輸	279	sī	嘶	2671	suǒ	所	857	táo	桃	224
shū	書	311	sī	撕	2672	suǒ	鎖	1590	táo	逃	1594
shū	叔	604	sǐ	死	664	suǒ	索	2327	táo	淘	2838
shū	梳	633	sì	四	4				táo	陶	2839
shū	樞	1252	sì	寺	155		T		táo	萄	2996
shū	淑	1852	sì	似	797				tǎo	討	324
shū	疏	1876	sì	飼	2758	tā	它	428	tào	套	1390
shū	蔬	1877	sì	肆	2805	tā	她	477	tè	特	236
shū	殊	1909	sōng	松	644	tā	他	752	téng	藤	2180
shū	舒	2211	sōng	鬆	2807	tā	塌	1745	téng	疼	2596
shǔ	屬	1482	sǒng	聳	2961	tǎ	塔	247	téng	騰	2847
shǔ	暑	2233	sòng	送	1440	tà	踏	2252	tī	梯	2223
						tāi	胎	1865			

tī	踢	2260	tú	徒	1931	wǎng	往	704	wò	沃	1669
tí	題	369	tú	屠	2241	wǎng	網	1021	wò	臥	2030
tí	提	563	tú	塗	2582	wǎng	枉	1580	wū	屋	824
tí	啼	1672	tú	涂	3015	wàng	妄	459	wū	巫	1460
tí	蹄	2254	tǔ	土	147	wàng	望	460	wū	烏	2818
tǐ	體	1070	tǔ	吐	151	wàng	忘	530	wū	嗚	2819
tì	替	681	tù	兔	1409	wàng	旺	1577	wū	污	2874
tì	惕	2078	tuán	團	1471	wēi	威	344	wū	誣	2938
tì	剃	2221	tuī	推	565	wēi	微	705	wú	吾	18
tì	涕	2222	tuí	頹	1942	wēi	危	1057	wú	無	1295
tiān	天	403	tuǐ	腿	1090	wéi	維	1007	wú	吳	1369
tiān	添	1773	tuì	退	1089	wéi	韋	1221	wǔ	五	5
tián	田	14	tūn	吞	1667	wéi	圍	1222	wǔ	武	360
tián	填	150	tún	屯	2472	wéi	唯	1731	wǔ	午	509
tián	甜	2663	tuō	脫	468	wéi	惟	1779	wǔ	舞	1294
tiáo	條	744	tuō	託	1384	wéi	違	2570	wǔ	伍	1990
tiǎo	挑	1809	tuō	拖	1817	wěi	委	719	wǔ	侮	2018
tiào	跳	975	tuō	托	2800	wěi	偉	1223	wù	勿	815
tiē	貼	52	tuǒ	妥	1859	wěi	尾	1382	wù	物	817
tiě	鐵	339	tuó	駝	2984	wěi	偽	1386	wù	務	934
tiě	帖	1657	tuò	拓	1803	wěi	萎	1947	wù	霧	935
tīng	聽	708	tuò	唾	2536	wěi	緯	2571	wù	誤	1371
tīng	廳	709				wèi	胃	28	wù	悟	1755
tíng	亭	299				wèi	未	202			
tíng	停	759	**W**			wèi	味	205			
tíng	廷	794	wā	哇	152	wèi	位	749	**X**		
tíng	庭	795	wā	蛙	1709	wèi	衛	1224	xī	夕	108
tíng	蜓	2986	wā	挖	2285	wèi	為	1385	xī	息	538
tǐng	挺	2064	wá	娃	1527	wèi	謂	1620	xī	吸	585
tǐng	艇	2761	wǎ	瓦	2065	wèi	慰	2105	xī	昔	897
tōng	通	1054	wà	襪	1649	wèi	蔚	2106	xī	希	1108
tóng	同	176	wāi	歪	2202	wèi	畏	2801	xī	稀	1109
tóng	銅	262	wài	外	111	wèi	喂	2802	xī	西	1191
tóng	童	414	wān	彎	1023	wèi	魏	3019	xī	熄	1786
tóng	桐	1552	wān	灣	1024	wēn	溫	1079	xī	熙	1919
tǒng	統	1010	wán	丸	41	wén	聞	1208	xī	膝	1951
tǒng	筒	1985	wán	頑	58	wén	文	1270	xī	錫	2077
tǒng	桶	2376	wán	完	182	wén	蚊	1271	xī	犀	2082
tòng	痛	1248	wán	玩	252	wén	紋	2651	xī	析	2121
tōu	偷	2011	wǎn	晚	1412	wěn	吻	2075	xī	晰	2122
tóu	投	597	wǎn	宛	2386	wěn	穩	2609	xī	惜	2171
tóu	頭	1067	wǎn	婉	2388	wèn	問	1204	xī	犧	2226
tòu	透	721	wǎn	碗	2389	wēng	翁	1891	xī	溪	2342
tū	凸	31	wǎn	挽	2843	wō	渦	2273	xī	嘻	2416
tū	突	997	wàn	萬	1401	wō	蝸	2275	xī	悉	2790
tū	禿	1941	wàn	腕	2387	wō	窩	2293	xí	習	512
tú	圖	522	wāng	汪	1579	wǒ	我	551	xí	席	904
tú	途	1235	wáng	王	248	wò	握	825	xí	襲	1445
			wáng	亡	457				xí	媳	1785

zhì	緻	2314	zhū	株	1558	zhuāng	裝	919	zōng	棕	2108
zhì	摯	2494	zhū	珠	1581	zhuāng	椿	2915	zōng	綜	2319
zhì	擲	2745	zhū	諸	2239	zhuàng	壯	917	zōng	蹤	2960
zhōng	中	36	zhū	蛛	2982	zhuàng	撞	1820	zǒng	總	1476
zhōng	鐘	415	zhú	竹	728	zhuàng	狀	2181	zòng	縱	1486
zhōng	終	1013	zhú	逐	1717	zhuī	追	962	zǒu	走	365
zhōng	衷	1652	zhú	燭	2955	zhuì	墜	2284	zòu	奏	2527
zhōng	忠	1756	zhǔ	主	259	zhuì	綴	2935	zū	租	2682
zhōng	鍾	2593	zhǔ	煮	2238	zhǔn	準	504	zú	族	928
zhǒng	種	1245	zhǔ	囑	2957	zhǔn	准	1739	zú	足	973
zhǒng	腫	2591	zhù	貯	190	zhuō	桌	211	zǔ	組	1299
zhòng	眾	784	zhù	注	260	zhuō	捉	2255	zǔ	祖	1300
zhòng	重	1242	zhù	住	748	zhuó	卓	47	zǔ	阻	2684
zhòng	仲	1994	zhù	助	1301	zhuó	灼	1531	zuàn	鑽	1591
zhōu	州	124	zhù	柱	1586	zhuó	啄	1722	zuǐ	嘴	1317
zhōu	洲	134	zhù	註	1626	zhuó	琢	1723	zuì	最	669
zhōu	周	305	zhù	築	1986	zhuó	酌	2394	zuì	罪	1214
zhōu	週	306	zhù	祝	2102	zhuó	濁	2954	zuì	醉	2398
zhōu	舟	1350	zhù	鑄	2754	zī	資	444	zūn	尊	1064
zhōu	粥	2218	zhù	駐	2851	zī	姿	445	zūn	遵	1065
zhóu	軸	2110	zhuā	抓	613	zī	諮	446	zuó	昨	867
zhǒu	肘	1530	zhuǎ	爪	612	zī	滋	2352	zuǒ	左	73
zhòu	咒	1567	zhuān	專	1468	zǐ	子	92	zuǒ	佐	2000
zhòu	晝	1612	zhuān	磚	2942	zǐ	仔	2001	zuò	做	746
zhòu	皺	1904	zhuàn	轉	1470	zǐ	姊	2227	zuò	坐	785
zhòu	宙	2109	zhuàn	賺	2145	zǐ	紫	2309	zuò	座	786
zhòu	驟	2864	zhuàn	撰	2705	zì	自	32	zuò	作	868
zhū	豬	961	zhuāng	妝	916	zì	字	180			
zhū	朱	1557	zhuāng	莊	918	zōng	宗	840			

INDEX V

Key Words and Primitive Meanings

This Index contains a cumulative list of all the key words and primitive meanings used in Books 1 and 2. Key words are listed with their respective character and frame number. Primitive meanings are listed in italics and are followed only by the number of the volume and the page (also in italics) on which they are first introduced.

shaker, salt		2.212	show	示	834	sing	唱	24
shallow	淺	351	show off	耀	2269	sinister	凶	1113
shame	恥	1914	shows	齣	2478	sink	淪	2720
shape	形	1262	*shredder*		2.90	sister, elder	姊	2227
sharp	銳	1706	shrimp	蝦	1359	sister, father's	姑	1514
shattered	碎	2401	shrink	縮	2318	sister, older	姐	1298
shave	剃	2221	shrug	聳	2961	sister, younger	妹	206
she	她	477	shun	忌	1778	sit	坐	785
sheaf		1.303	shut	關	1457	site	場	493
shears	剪	278	shuteye, get some	寢	2184	situation	況	143
shed	棚	1542	shuttle	梭	2403	six	六	6
sheep	羊	495	shy	羞	2966	skeleton	骨	978
shelf	架	697	sick and tired of	膩	1630	skill	技	602
shell	殼	1962	sickle	鐮	2150	skin	膚	2868
shell, spiral	螺	2296	*sickness*		1.329	skirt	裙	885
shell out	繳	2330	side	旁	466	sky, red	霞	2770
shellfish	貝	51	side by side	並	1302	skyscraper	廈	1753
shells		1.41	*side by side and*			slanting	斜	2583
shelter	蔽	1981	*upside down*		1.340	slaughter	屠	2241
shelves		1.338	side room	廂	1750	*slaughterhouse*		1.130
Shen	沈	3006	sides, press from			slave	奴	693
shield	盾	1855	both	夾	2043	*sled dogs*		1.251
shift	移	713	*siesta*		1.247	sleep	睡	1185
shiny	亮	300	*sieve*		1.343	sleeping, for	臥	2030
ship	船	1351	sift	篩	2245	sleeve	袖	2111
ship's cabin	艙	2763	sigh	嘆	2532	slice	片	914
shirt	衫	2641	sigh—ay-ay	唉	2205	slide	溜	1047
shocking	覊	1582	sight, keep out of	匿	2622	slight	薄	2731
shoes	鞋	1366	sign	簽	2055	slightly	稍	1944
shoot	射	952	sign of the			*slingshot*		1.278
shoot		1.257	dragon	辰	1436	slip, bamboo	籤	2565
shoot, bamboo	筍	1984	sign of the pig	亥	1136	slippery	滑	979
shop	鋪	2725	sign of the tiger	寅	1434	slope	坡	1901
shop, butcher		1.130	*sign of Zorro*		1.272	slow	慢	675
shore	岸	1226	*silage*		1.316	slowly	徐	2580
short	短	1068	silent	默	227	slumber	眠	1335
short of, fall	差	501	silk	絲	1005	slump	跌	2258
short of stature	矮	2204	silk fabric	綢	2306	sly	狡	2250
should	該	1140	silk gauze	羅	1008	small	小	103
shoulder	肩	2094	silkworm	蠶	2462	small bell	鈴	2373
shoulder, carry			silver	銀	1083	small box	盒	2422
over the	扛	1798	*silver*		1.299	small cup	盞	2421
shoulders, drape			similar	似	797	small objects	枚	1615
over the	披	1902	simple	簡	1206	small plum	梅	432
shout	呼	1107	simulate	擬	2371	small shovel	鏟	2652
shovel	鍬	1964	since	既	1101	*small table*		1.40
shovel, small	鏟	2652	sincere	誠	343	smart	聰	2948

smash	砸	2618	sound	音	449	spokes	輻	1599
smear	塗	2582	soup	湯	494	*spool*		*1.289*
smear on	抹	1806	sour	酸	2402	spoon	匙	1676
smelt	冶	1866	source	源	140	spoon, ancient	匕	419
smidgen	釐	1614	south	南	1200	spot	點	173
smoke	煙	1199	sovereign	帝	413	spotless	潔	2520
smooth	暢	2115	*sow*		*1.195*	spread	傳	1469
smoothly, go	亨	1607	sow	栽	1635	spring	泉	129
snail	蝸	2275	spacious	敞	319	springtime	春	1171
snake		*1.194*	spare	饒	2452	sprinkle	澆	1533
snake hook		*2.218*	spare time	暇	2769	sprout	芽	2782
snakeskin		*1.194*	*sparkler*		*1.334*	*sprout*		*1.257*
snare		*1.276*	sparkling	晶	22	spurt	噴	1833
sniff	嗅	1570	*sparks*		*1.67*	spy	探	1002
snitch		*1.375*	sparrow	雀	1740	square	矩	2614
snot	涕	2222	sparse	疏	1876	squat	蹲	2410
snow	雪	869	speak	說	469	squeeze	擠	2964
snowflake		*1.70*	spear	矛	931	squint	睞	1978
snowman		*1.263*	*spear, ceremonial*		*1.274*	St. Bernard dog		*1.63*
so far	迄	1685	special	特	236	St. Gobbler		*2.60*
soak	沾	1523	specialty	專	1468	stable	穩	2609
soap	皂	35	species	種	1245	stagnant	滯	391
soar	翔	513	speck	斑	2650	stairs	階	994
society	社	835	speech, figure of	喻	1601	*stairway to*		
socks	襪	1649	speedy	迅	270	*heaven*		*1.354*
soft	軟	442	Sphinx	斯	1290	stake	樁	2915
soil	土	147	spice plant	椒	1853	*stalk, rice*		*1.307*
soldier	士	307	spicy hot	辣	1238	*stamp*		*1.292*
soldiers, foot		*2.150*	spider (back end)	蛛	2982	*stamp collection*		*1.330*
solely	唯	1731	spider (front end)	蜘	2981	stand, vendor's	攤	1180
solemn	肅	2195	*spike*		*1.55*	standard	準	504
solicit	徵	1933	spill	灑	2891	standing grain	禾	710
solid	固	515	spin	紡	2311	standing up	立	408
solitary	寞	1564	spinach	菠	1907	*staple gun*		*1.349*
somebody	身	951	*spinach*		*1.315*	*staples*		*1.295*
someone	者	959	spine	呂	800	star	星	1164
someone sitting			spiral shell	螺	2296	stare at	盯	1510
on the ground		*1.173*	spirit	靈	1461	start	倡	1992
somewhat	些	427	spirit, evil	祟	2101	startled	驚	1421
Song	宋	1553	spit	吐	151	starving	飢	2451
song	歌	441	splash	潑	2637	state	州	124
son-in-law	婿	1647	splatter	濺	1639	state of affairs	狀	2181
sore	瘡	2607	spleen	脾	2968	*state of mind*		*1.204*
sorry about, be	悔	1774	splendid	熙	1919	station	站	410
sort	般	1352	splendor	華	1181	stationed, be	駐	2851
sort of thing	然	228	split	劈	2487	stature, short of	矮	2204
soul	魂	2902	spoiled	爛	1483	stay	留	1046

stay overnight	宿	2008	*streetwalker*		*2.151*	*sunflower*			*1.28*
steal	偷	2011	strengthen	鞏	2775	*sunglasses*			*2.220*
steam	蒸	1373	stretch	張	1388	sunny	晴		2506
steel	鋼	2826	*stretch*		*1.158*	*sunrise, sunset*			*1.92*
steep	陡	2279	strict	嚴	673	sunset	暮		1565
stele	碑	2970	stride	邁	1402	superb	佳		2005
stem, fruit	蒂	1673	strike	打	559	superfluous	冗		288
stem, plant	莖	2339	string together	串	1504	superintend	督		605
step on	踩	2256	stringed			supervise	監		1080
stepladder		*1.331*	instrument	琴	2539	supplement	輔		2726
stern	屬	2824	strive	勉	2844	supplicate	祈		2130
stew	熬	1701	stroll	逛	273	supply	供		1307
stick, thick	槓	1544	strong	強	943	support	持		561
stick, walking		*1.32*	stronghold	塞	2503	surface	表		1161
stick horse		*1.199*	-struct	附	2998	*surfboarding*			*2.119*
sticky	黏	1948	struggle	掙	2153	surging	滔		2928
stiff	僵	2216	stubborn	頑	58	surname	姓		1165
still	仍	751	stuck, get	陷	2929	surpass	越		367
sting	叮	87	study	學	1110	surprised	訝		2783
stinking	臭	231	*study group*		*2.194*	surround	圍		1222
stir	攪	1112	stuff	材	1836	survey	勘		2674
stir up trouble	鬧	1663	stuffy	悶	2553	suspend	懸		1463
stir-fry	炒	1532	stunned	愕	2875	swallow	燕		2174
stitching		*1.371*	stupid	笨	1987	swamp	澤		2492
stockade	寨	2504	style	式	333	swan	鴻		2810
stockpile	屯	2472	submerge	潛	2461	sway	晃		1520
stolen goods	贓	2187	submit	呈	256	sweat	汗		2577
stomach	胃	28	substitute for	代	769	sweep	掃		873
stone	石	114	succor	贊	1573	sweet	甘		1285
stoop	躬	2230	such and such	某	1286	swell	漲		1389
stop	止	353	sudden, all of a	恍	1761	swim	泳		133
stop up	堵	2237	suddenly	忽	816	swimming, go	游		813
storage, put in	儲	2240	suffer	挨	2207	swindle	詐		2135
store	店	523	suffering	苦	214	swing	盪		2424
store up	貯	190	sufficient	充	630	swollen	腫		2591
storehouse	倉	1209	(suffix)	麼	1038	sword	刀		79
stork		*1.216*	sugar	糖	880	symbol	符		2038
story	層	828	sugary	甜	2663	system	制		393
stove	爐	2870	suitable	適	417				
straddle	跨	2878	sulfur	硫	1874	**T**			
straight	直	68	sum up	綜	2319	table	桌		211
strait	窄	2289	summer	夏	285	*table*			*1.297*
strange	奇	122	summer heat	暑	2233	*table, small*			*1.40*
strategy	策	735	summon	召	82	tactful	婉		2388
stream	川	123	*sun*		*1.23*	tail	尾		1382
streamer	幟	453	sun, rising	旭	26	tailor	裁		1648
street	街	706	*Sunday school*		*2.140*	Taiwan	臺		1871